S0-BKO-305

What Everyone Needs
To Know About
GOD

By
Don Stewart

What Everyone Needs To Know About God

Published by Dart Press
Box 6486
Orange, California 92613

ISBN   1-877825-06-9

All Rights Reserved. No portion of this book may be reproduced in any form without the written permission of the Publisher.

PRINTED IN THE UNITED STATES OF AMERICA BY
GILLILAND PRINTING INC.
215 NORTH SUMMIT
ARKANSAS CITY, KANSAS 67005

All Scripture quotations are from the New King James Version unless otherwise noted.

What Everyone Needs To Know About GOD

By
Don Stewart

Contents

Part II   God: His Nature

Part III   God: His Acts

Part IV   God: His Meaning To The Individual

Summary

INTRODUCTION

Does God exist? If He does exist what is He like? Is it possible for anyone to know Him? Questions such as these have troubled man from the beginning of time. He wants to know if there exists a being greater than himself.

The Bible says there is a God who exists and it tells us what He is like, what He has done in history, and how He relates to us as individuals. It provides for us answers to three of man's most important questions, "Who am I? Why do I exist? What is going to happen to me when I die?"

Using the Bible as its source, this book will answer many common questions that people often ask about God. It is meant as an introductory work to give people a basic idea of what Christians believe about God and why they believe it.

Format

The book is divided into four sections. Each section will build upon the previous ones.

The first section deals with the existence of God. Does God exist? Is there evidence for His existence that a person can investigate? How do we know that He exists?

Once the case for God's existence is established we will move on to His character. What is God like? Does He have a body? Is God love? Is God the Father of all mankind?

After establishing what the Bible says about the character of God we will examine God working in history. The Bible teaches that God has revealed Himself in the past. How are we to understand what He has done? If God is good then why is there evil in the world? Why did He create hell? Why doesn't He reveal Himself to everyone?

The last section will deal with God and the individual. Can a person know God? What does God require of a person? Must someone have great faith or works to please God? Does God answer prayer? Will God accept everyone?

Why Should We Learn About God?

When people talk about God, the term *theology* is often used. *Theology* means "the study of God." It comes from two Greek words, *theos* meaning God, *logos* meaning "the study of something."

Theology includes the study of God and His relationship to the universe. When a person asks questions about God he is asking questions about theology.

There are several purposes for studying theology:

Understand the Faith

The believer studies theology in order to define his Christian faith. It is difficult to have a personal relationship with someone you do not know. A person must understand what he believes about God and how God relates to mankind and the universe. This is in order to understand God's purpose for us while we live here on earth. The Apostle Paul said his overwhelming desire was to know God:

> That I may know Him and the power of His resurrection, and the fellowship of His sufferings, being conformed to His death (Philippians 3:10).

Defend the Truth

When a believer is proclaiming God's truth to others he is often asked many questions by those who do not believe. A proper understanding of theology can help the believer answer the questions accurately and intelligently. The Bible commands us to know what we believe and why we believe it.

> But sanctify the Lord God in your hearts, and always be ready to give a defense to everyone who asks you a reason for the hope that is in you, with meekness and fear (1 Peter 3:15).

Spread the Message

The study of theology is also necessary for the spreading of the Christian message. Christ told His disciples to tell the whole world the good news about him:

> Go therefore and make disciples of all the nations, baptizing them in the name of the Father and of the Son and of the Holy Spirit (Matthew 28:19).

This Good News can only be proclaimed when properly understood.

The Bible encourages people to use their minds, with reasonable faith, when investigating the claims for God's existence and His works: "Test all things; hold fast to what is good" (1 Thessalonians 5:21).

We invite the reader to consider what the Bible claims about the God it reveals.

PART 1

GOD: HIS EXISTENCE

You are My witnesses, says the Lord, And My servant whom I have chosen, that you may know and believe Me, and understand that I am He. Before Me there was no God formed, nor shall there be after Me.

—Isaiah 43:10

WHO IS GOD?

The most frequently asked questions about God concern His identity. Who is God? What is He like?

Our information about God is derived from four sources: nature, the spirit and mind of man, the Bible, and the person of Jesus Christ. From these sources we can have a basic, though not complete, picture of the nature of God.

Eternal

God is eternal. He has always existed and He will always exist. There has never been a time when God did not exist.

God is Spirit

God's form is that of a spirit. He is an invisible eternal spirit.

Perfect

God is absolute perfection. He does not need anything or anyone to exist. He is complete within Himself. He is the perfect, eternal spirit.

The Only God

He is the only God who exists. There is no other God, either more or less powerful.

Personal

God is also personal. This means that He has intelligence, will, emotion, and self-cognizance. He is not some vague creative force.

A basic definition of God from the preceding statements includes these facts: God is a personal, eternal spirit who is absolute perfection. He is the only God that has existed or that ever will exist.

With this as a starting point we will now consider questions about God and His character.

WHO CREATED GOD? WHERE DID HE COME FROM?

People continue to ask age-old questions about the origin of God. Who created God?—that is assuming that He does exist? Where did He come from? How did He get to be God? Did He have a beginning? Did He have parents?

No Beginning

Nobody created God. He is by nature the eternal God. He was not created at all. He always was, is, and always will be. He did not work Himself up into a position to be God neither did He inherit the position from His parents, for He had no parents—no mother, no father. He has no beginning and will have no end. The fact that God is eternal is stressed in the Bible.

The psalmist wrote:

Even from everlasting to everlasting You are God (Psalm 90:2).

In the Book of Deuteronomy God said:

For I lift My hand to heaven, and say, as I live forever (Deuteronomy 32:40).

Arguing in a Circle?

Some might argue that these statements "beg the question" for they are assuming what they should be proving. They conveniently start with God but do not explain the how or why of His existence.

But the starting point, according to the Bible is God. God was in the beginning and everything stems from Him.

IS GOD DEAD?

During the mid-1960's there was much interest in a philosophical movement that believed that God was dead. Is God dead? The question is a valid one and the answer is no. God is alive and working His will in the universe.

Then why don't we hear from Him? Why is God silent? Why doesn't He reveal Himself so everyone can see Him?

He is Not Silent

The Bible says God has spoken. He has revealed Himself in history. Each page of the Old and New Testaments gives evidence of God revealing Himself. The climax to God's revelation was when He became a man in the person of Jesus Christ.

> God, who at various times and in different ways spoke in time past to the fathers by the prophets, has in these last days spoken to us by His Son, whom He has appointed heir of all things, through whom also He made the worlds (Hebrews 1:1,2).

Since the time of Christ and the writing of the New Testament documents, there have been no additional revelations from God. The writing of inspired Scripture ended with the writings of Christ's apostles and their disciples.

The next time God will publicly intervene in the affairs of man is when He comes again in the person of Jesus Christ. At that time every eye shall see Him.

Behold, He is coming with clouds, and every eye shall
see Him, and they also who pierced Him. And all the tribes
of the earth will mourn because of Him (Revelation 1:7).

Patience of God

The silence of God is a testimony to His patience. God is
still waiting for people to repent of their sins:

The Lord is not slack concerning His promise, as some
count slackness, but is longsuffering toward us, not
willing that any should perish but that all should come to
repentance (2 Peter 3:9).

But if God showed Himself today would it cause people
to believe? No. Though people would not be able to deny
God's existence, His presence would not cause everyone to
trust Him. It is one thing believing that God exists, it is
quite another thing to make a trusting commitment to
Him.

Jesus, in His day, demonstrated beyond any doubt
that He was the Messiah, the One sent from God the
Father to save the world. Yet the majority of people
attributed His miracles to the devil and finally crucified
Him. This was not because of lack of evidence. It was
because they did not want to believe.

Although people today might say that they would
become believers if God personally appeared to them, this
is not necessarily the case. The problem is not so much a
matter of evidence as it is a matter of the human heart. The
prophet Jeremiah said:

The heart is deceitful above all things, and desperately
wicked; who can know it? (Jeremiah 17:9).

Even if God were to appear publicly it would not cause
an outpouring of faith toward Him.

The Bible says that God lives and that He is still
working His plan for the universe. And though God is not
giving any further revelation of Himself, He is still working
in the hearts and lives of mankind.

WHAT IS GOD'S NATURE?

God, by nature is a Triune Being or Trinity. The Trinity, simply stated, is as follows: The Bible teaches that there is one eternal God who is the Creator and Sustainer of the universe. He is the only God that exists. Within the nature of this one God are three eternal persons, The Father, the Son, and the Holy Spirit. These three persons are the one God. The Trinity doctrine is based on what the Scripture says concerning the nature of God.

One God

A point that the Scripture clearly establishes is that there is only one God who exists:

Hear, O Israel: The Lord our God, the Lord is one (Deuteronomy 6:4).

For there is one God (1 Timothy 2:5).

'Thus says the Lord,' the King of Israel, and His redeemer, the Lord of hosts: 'I am the First and I am the Last: besides Me there is no God' (Isaiah 43:10).

These passages and many other Biblical statements make it clear that there is only one God.

Plurality of Persons

Even though only one God exists we are told in Scripture that there is a plurality of persons in His being or nature. God said

Let Us make man in Our image, according to Our likeness (Genesis 1:26).

God also said:

Behold, the man has become like one of Us (Genesis 3:22).

These verses allude to God's plurality of persons. We know that God could not be talking to angels here for angels did not, nor could they, help God create the universe.

This plurality, however, is not the same as a split personality or insanity. There are three separate personalities within the nature of the one God.

God the Father

The Bible talks about a person who is designated as the Father. This person is called God. Isaiah the prophet wrote:

But now, O Lord, you are our Father (Isaiah 64:8).

Jesus taught His disciples to pray: "Our Father in heaven" (Matthew 6:9).

When the Apostle Paul wrote to the Christians in Galatia, he began his letter,

Paul, an Apostle (not from men nor through man, but through Jesus Christ and God the Father who raised Him from the dead) (Galatians 1:1).

God is called the Father in both the Old and New Testaments.

God the Son

The Bible records the existence of a second person who is distinct from the Father and who is also called God. This person is Jesus, God the Son. John the evangelist wrote:

In the beginning was the Word, and the Word was with God, and the Word was God (John 1:1).

In another place John wrote:

Therefore the Jews sought all the more to kill Him, because He not only broke the Sabbath, but also said that God was His Father, making Himself equal with God (John 5:18).

The New Testament makes it clear that Jesus is God.

God the Holy Spirit

There is a third Person revealed in the Bible who is different from both the Father and the Son. He is known as the Holy Spirit. The Holy Spirit is also referred to as being God.

Ananias, why has Satan filled your heart to lie to the Holy Spirit?. . . You have not lied to men, but to God (Acts 5:3,4 Revised Standard Version).

To understand the doctrine of the Trinity key facts must be kept in mind:

1. The Bible teaches that there is only one God.

2. Biblical statements allude to the plurality of persons within God's nature.

3. The Scripture also says that there are three distinct persons, The Father, the Son, and the Holy Spirit. Each of these three persons are called God.

4. Since there is only one God and since the Father, the Son, and the Holy Spirit are all called God, the inescapable conclusion is that these three persons are the one God. This is the doctrine of the Trinity.

HOW HAS GOD REVEALED HIMSELF?

The Bible says that God has revealed Himself to mankind in four different ways. They include (1) Nature (2) Man's conscience (3) Jesus Christ (4) The Bible.

Nature

The universe with its vastness and complexity gives testimony to God and His glory. The Bible says:

> When I consider Your heavens, the work of Your fingers, the moon and the stars, which You have ordained, what is man that You are mindful of him (Psalm 8:3,4).

Yet the testimony of nature only tells us about God in a limited way. The Book of Job states this fact.

> He binds up the water in His thick clouds, yet the clouds are not broken under it. He covers the face of His throne, and spreads His cloud over it . . . Indeed these are the mere edges of His ways, and how small a whisper we hear of Him! But the thunder of His power who can understand (Job 26:8,9,14).

But that which we can know about God leaves us without any excuses.

For since the creation of the world His invisible attributes are clearly seen, being understood by the things that are made, even His eternal power and Godhead, so that they are without excuse (Romans 1:20).

Man's Conscience

God has also revealed Himself through the spirit, or mind, of man. All societies have a certain moral code built into them in which stealing, lying, murder, and such are universally condemned. Man's sense of right and wrong testifies to God's existence. The Apostle Paul wrote:

For when Gentiles, who do not have the law, by nature do the things contained in the law, these although not having the law are a law to themselves, who show the work of the law written in their hearts, their conscience also bearing witness, and between themselves their thoughts accusing or else excusing them (Romans 2:14,15).

Jesus Christ

God has also revealed Himself to the world through the person of Jesus Christ.

God, who at various times and in different ways spoke in time past to the fathers by the prophets, has in these last days spoken to us by His Son, whom He has appointed heir of all things, through whom also He made the worlds (Hebrews 1:1,2).

Jesus Himself testified that He had come to earth to reveal the will of God the Father.

All things have been delivered to Me by My Father, and no one knows the Son except the Father. Nor does anyone know the Father except the Son, and he to whom the Son wills to reveal Him (Matthew 11:27).

The Scriptures

God also has revealed Himself through the written Word, the Scriptures. The Bible is God's revelation of Himself to mankind. The Scripture says of itself:

All Scripture is given by inspiration of God, and is profitable for doctrine, for reproof for correction, for instruction in righteousness (2 Timothy 3:16).

God has given man ample opportunity to know about Him by means of nature, the conscience of man, Jesus Christ, and through the Bible.

WHY SHOULD WE EXPECT GOD TO REVEAL HIMSELF?

The idea that God should reveal Himself to mankind is not an unreasonable position. When one examines the situation it makes sense that God would reveal Himself.

Possible

First, it is possible that God could reveal Himself. If God exists as the Creator of the universe, it is certainly possible that He would reveal Himself. He has the ability to communicate Himself to man. This being the case, there is nothing that rules out the possibility of God revealing Himself.

Probable

Furthermore, it is probable that God would reveal Himself. He has made man a personal being with the ability to communicate with others. Since God has made man this way why shouldn't He communicate with His creation?

Love

Another reason that we should expect God to reveal Himself is because He loves us. Love needs to be shared.

Expected

We should expect, therefore, that a divine revelation be given. Since there is nothing stopping God from revealing Himself and since He has made man with the ability to give and receive communication, a divine revelation is consistent with what we know about God.

Necessary

From mankind's position, it is necessary that God reveal Himself. We can know many things about God from nature. The fact that He is the Creator, and the fact that His creation is wonderfully made is obvious to all. Yet nature does not tell us what God wants us to do. We need a divine revelation to know and understand who God is and what He wants from us. Thus a supernatural revelation from God to us is not only possible, but from man's point of view it is essential.

Therefore we conclude;

1. A supernatural communication from God to man is not unreasonable.

2. If God exists it is certainly possible that He could reveal Himself.

3. Because God has made men as personal beings who communicate with one another it is probable that He would communicate with His creation.

4. God loves us and wants to communicate His love to us.

5. From mankind's point of view it is necessary for God to reveal Himself to us.

WHAT CLASSICAL ARGUMENTS ARE GIVEN TO SHOW THAT GOD EXISTS?

There are many reasons we believe that God exists. They include the following:

Classical Arguments

Three of the classical arguments given for the existence of God are the cosmological, the teleological, the moral argument. Simply stated they are as follows:

Cosmological Argument

The cosmological argument argues that there must be a sufficient cause or a reason for the universe (cosmos). Every effect has a cause. The universe is an effect. There must be a first cause, an uncaused cause, and that cause must be God.

Teleological Argument

The teleological argument, from the Greek word *telos*, meaning "purpose, end, or goal," is an argument from design and purpose. Everything in the universe has a purpose. The original or ultimate designer or purposer is God. The psalmist pointed out this fact.

He waters the hills from the upper chambers; the earth is satisfied with the fruit of Your works. He causes the grass to grow for cattle, and vegetation for the service of man, that he may bring forth food from the earth, and wine that makes glad the heart of man, oil to make his face shine, and bread which strengthens man's heart (Psalm 104:14,15).

If everything observable has a design and purpose then why not the universe itself?

Moral Argument

The moral argument states that there must be a God to account for the sense of right and wrong that is universal within man. Every human culture has some moral standards. The reason man has moral standards is because the Creator put that within him. This human moral sense points to the existence of God. The Bible says:

For when Gentiles, who do not have the law, by nature do the things contained in the law, these, although not having the law, are a law to themselves, who show the work of the law written in their hearts, their conscience also bearing witness, and between themselves their thoughts accusing or excusing them (Romans 2:14,15).

These arguments have been used down through the centuries to show that belief in the existence of God is not something illogical, but that God's existence best explains the universe in which we live.

Other Evidence

There is other evidence existing that gives us reason to believe that God exists. This includes the Bible, predictive prophecy, Jesus Christ, and changed lives of believers.

These arguments have been used down through the centuries to show that belief in the existence of God is not something illogical, but that it best explains the universe in which we live.

DOES THE BIBLE GIVE EVIDENCE AS BEING THE WORD OF GOD?

One of the reasons we can have confidence that God exists is the Bible. The Bible is like no other book that has ever been written before or since. It claims to be the inspired Word of God, and has more proof for that claim than any other book.

All Scripture is given by inspiration of God, and is profitable for doctrine, for reproof, for correction, for instruction in righteousness (2 Timothy 3:16).

But the mere claim of divine inspiration does not make it true. There has to be evidence to back up the claim, and the evidence for the inspiration of the Bible is sufficient to the reasonable questioner.

The Bible, though made up of sixty-six separate books, is in reality one book. One of the strongest arguments for the inspiration of the Bible is its unity.

Fifteen Hundred Years in the Making

The first book of the Bible written was either Genesis or Job (about 1400 B.C.). The last book composed was either the third letter of John or the Book of Revelation. They each were written toward the end of the first century A.D. This makes a total of about fifteen hundred years from the composition of the first book of the Bible until the last.

Many Authors, Many Occupations

In addition, there were over forty different authors who composed the books of the Bible. They came from a variety of backgrounds and different occupations. For example, Amos was a herdsman, Peter and John were fishermen, Luke was a doctor, Joshua, a military leader, and Daniel a prime minister.

Three Languages

The Bible was written in three different languages—Hebrew, Aramaic, and Greek; and upon three different continents—Africa, Asia, and Europe.

Different Subjects

The subject matter contained in the Bible includes many controversial matters including the existence and nature of God, the formation of the universe, the creation and purpose of man.

Harmony

Thus the Bible is sixty-six books, composed by forty different human authors, over a fifteen-hundred-year span, written in three different continents, covering many controversial subjects. One would expect the result to be a confused and disjointed text, anything but harmonious. Yet the Bible is a unity. It is one unfolding story from beginning to end written with complete harmony and continuity. This feature is remarkable when one considers the different factors involved. The only reasonable way that this Book came together so precisely is that the ultimate author behind it was God Himself.

Hence, the Bible itself gives us reason to believe in the existence of God. (For more information on the reliability of the Bible, see Don Stewart, *Ten Reasons To Trust The Bible*, Orange, California, Dart Press, 1990, and *What Everyone Needs To Know About The Bible*, Orange, California, Dart Press, 1992).

HOW DOES PREDICTIVE PROPHECY GIVE EVIDENCE FOR GOD'S EXISTENCE?

The Scripture records many events that were predicted in advance by God. These fulfilled prophecies are evidence of God's knowledge of all things. Only God, who is outside of our time-space existence and our finite knowledge, could accurately and consistently reveal the future. The Bible says,

> We also have the prophetic word made more sure, which you do well to heed as a light that shines in a dark place, until the day dawns and the morning star rises in your hearts; knowing this first, that no prophecy of Scripture is of any private interpretation, for prophecy never came by the will of man, but holy men of God spoke as they were moved by the Holy Spirit (2 Peter 1:19-21).

Prophecy is God foretelling events before they occur. Biblical predictions are not vague prophecies but are specific in nature. Furthermore, they cannot be accounted for by chance, common sense, or collusion.

The Old Testament, for example, predicts the coming of a Savior known as the Messiah. The predictions surrounding Him are very specific. They include:

Birthplace

He was to be born in Bethlehem.

But you, Bethlehem Ephrathah, though you are little among the thousands of Judah, yet out of you shall come forth One to be ruler in Israel, whose goings forth have been from old, from everlasting (Micah 5:2).

Family Line

The Old Testament predicted the exact family line that the Messiah would come through. This includes the line of Abraham (Genesis 22:18), the line of Isaac (Genesis 21:12), the line of Jacob (Numbers 24:17), the family line of Jesse (Isaiah 11:1), and the line of David (Jeremiah 23:5).

Before Temple Destroyed

The Messiah was to come on the historical scene before the temple in Jerusalem was destroyed.

And after the sixty-two weeks Messiah shall be cut off, but not for Himself; and the people of the prince who is to come shall destroy the city and the sanctuary (Daniel 9:26).

The temple was destroyed in A.D. 70. Thus the predicted Messiah was prophesied to come upon the scene of history before A.D. 70.

Literally Fulfilled in Jesus

The odds that one person could fulfill these prophecies by chance are astronomical. But Jesus of Nazareth fulfilled these and many others demonstrating He was the promised Messiah.

Other Prophecies

The Bible also gives many prophecies concerning nations and individuals, which have been literally fulfilled. These also demonstrate that God exists and that He is controlling history.

Why Has He Told Us the Future?

Since the Bible gives us examples of God predicting the future we may rightly ask why He does this? Why has God at times predicted future events? Through the prophet Isaiah God gives us the answer to this question:

> Remember the former things of old, for I am God, and there is no other; I am God, and there is none like Me, declaring the end from the beginning, and from ancient times things that are not yet done, saying, 'My counsel shall stand, and I will do all My pleasure' (Isaiah 46:9,10).

> I have declared the former things from the beginning; they went forth from My mouth, and I caused them to hear it. Suddenly I did them, and they came to pass . . . Even from the beginning I have declared it to you; before it came to pass I proclaimed it to you, lest you should say, 'My idol has done them, and my carved image and my molded image have commanded them' (Isaiah 48:3,5).

From these verses we can deduce the following:

1. By telling us what is going to happen in the future we know that God exists for only God could know with certainty what will happen.

2. We can also know that He is the only God who exists for no other God or idol has been able to foretell the future with complete accuracy.

3. Man can also rest assured that other predictions God has made, which have come to pass, will indeed be fulfilled.

4. We can also trust anything else that God says because He has given us a basis for trusting Him.

5. We can, therefore, have confidence that God is controlling history and our own lives. By realizing that God has predicted the future accurately we can live in the security of what He has told us will happen.

Fulfilled biblical prophecy is convincing evidence of God's knowledge of all things—past, present, and future. (For more information on how the Bible predicts the future, see Don Stewart, *What The Bible Says About The Future*, Orange, California, Dart Press, 1992)

HOW DOES JESUS CHRIST TESTIFY TO GOD'S EXISTENCE?

The New Testament declares that Jesus Christ is the incarnation of the one true God.

The Gospel of John begins by stating the eternal nature of Jesus.

In the beginning was the Word, and the Word was with God, and the Word was God. . . And the Word became flesh and dwelt among us (John 1:14).

Here is the clear testimony that Jesus, the eternal God, became a man.

The Jews were offended at Jesus' claim to be God.

Therefore the Jews sought all the more to kill Him, because He not only broke the Sabbath, but also said that God was His Father, making Himself equal with God (John 5:18).

The fact that Jesus claimed to be God is clear, but were His claims true? Jesus gave evidence that He was God by doing the things only God could do. This included healing incurable diseases and raising the dead. His coming to earth fulfilled a number of prophecies that could not have been fulfilled by mere chance.

Jesus did something else only God could do, He forgave sin. Jesus said to a paralyzed man who was brought to Him, "Son, your sins are forgiven you" (Mark 2:5).

This claim brought a heated response from the religious leaders:

Why does this Man speak blasphemies like this? Who can forgive sins but God alone? (Mark 2:7).

They were absolutely right. Only God has the ability to forgive sins. The prophet Isaiah records God as saying,

I, even I, am He who blots out your transgressions for My own sake; and I will not remember your sins (Isaiah 43:25).

Jesus, by claiming the ability to forgive sin, put Himself on an equal level with God.

Conquering Death

Jesus' greatest feat, however, was conquering the greatest enemy we all face, death. The Bible says that the resurrection demonstrated that Jesus was God the Son.

And declared to be the Son of God with power, according to the Spirit of holiness, by the resurrection from the dead (Romans 1:4).

The death of Christ on the cross and His resurrection from the dead is the gospel, or Good News, in which we place our faith.

Moreover, brethren, I declare to you the gospel which I preached to you, which also you received and in which you stand . . . For I delivered to you first of all that which I received: that Christ died for our sins according to the Scriptures, and that He was buried, and that He rose again the third day according to the Scriptures (1 Corinthians 15:1,3,4).

The resurrection of Jesus demonstrated the fact that He is God. It showed that He has authority in all matters including life and death. (For more information about the evidence for the resurrection or Jesus, see Don Stewart, *What Everyone Needs To Know About Jesus*, Orange, California, Dart Press, 1992).

Therefore we can sum up the matter as follows:

1. The New Testament testifies that Jesus is the eternal God.

2. Jesus demonstrated that He could do the things only God could do, including conquering death.

3. Jesus' resurrection is evidence that He indeed was God the Son.

11

WHAT DOES THE TESTIMONY OF CHANGED LIVES TELL US ABOUT GOD?

There is, as we have seen, much objective evidence to tell us that God exists. There is a final line of evidence and that is the testimony of changed lives.

The Bible encourages people to experience God.

Oh, taste and see that the Lord is good; blessed is the man who trusts in Him! (Psalm 34:8).

Christian experience does not in and of itself prove the reality of the Christian faith. Yet if God has revealed Himself in the Bible, we should expect Christian experience to provide a testimony consistent with that revelation.

Jesus' Disciples

The disciples of Jesus are an example of experience validating God's Word. They all abandoned Jesus when He was betrayed by Judas Iscariot. Simon Peter even denied knowing Him. When Jesus was tried and crucified His disciples were nowhere to be found. Yet, less than two months later these same cowards were boldly proclaiming the truth of Christ to the world. They testified that seeing Jesus risen from the dead is what made the difference. Each one of these men suffered persecution the rest of his life and, with the exception of John, went on to die a martyr's death for his belief in Christ.

Seeing the Risen Christ

Something changed their lives. Cowards do not become martyrs without a reason. What was it? The disciples testified that it was seeing the risen Christ that made the difference. This was an historical event, not just a fairy tale. The Apostle Peter declared,

> For we did not follow cunningly devised fables when we made known to you the power and coming of our Lord Jesus Christ, but were eyewitnesses of His majesty. For He received from God the Father honor and glory, when such a voice came to Him from the Excellent Glory: 'This is My beloved Son, in whom I am well pleased.' And we heard this voice which came from heaven when we were with Him on the holy mountain (2 Peter 1:16-18).

Saul of Tarsus

The changed life of Jesus' disciples serve as a testimony to the truth of the Christian message. Saul of Tarsus is another example. He was a persecutor of Christians, but his life changed when he experienced the risen Christ while on the road to Damascus. This was a genuine experience, not a fantasy. He told King Agrippa,

> For the king, before whom I also speak freely, knows these things; for I am convinced that none of these things escapes his attention, since this thing was not done in a corner (Acts 26:26).

As was the case with Jesus' disciples, there is no disputing that Saul's life was radically changed. Like the disciples, he testified that it was caused by seeing the risen Christ. His changed life adds another testimony to the truth of the Christian faith.

Millions More

Since the time of Christ, there have been millions of others who have had their lives changed by experiencing the risen Christ. The experience of those who have believed in Christ is further confirmation of the truth of the Christian message.

We may conclude:

1. Christian experience is based upon the facts of the gospel.

2. The disciples of Jesus and Saul of Tarsus are two biblical examples of the confirmation of Christian experience.

3. Millions of others since the disciples have had the same experience.

4. Thus Christian experience gives a further confirmation of the truth of the Christian message.

WHAT DOES NATURE TELL US ABOUT GOD?

Does nature, that is the universe around us, tell us anything about God? Can we find evidence of God's existence from looking at the world in which we live?

The Bible asserts that the universe is a testimony to God's existence and precision. The psalmist had this to say:

The heavens declare the glory of God; and the firmament shows His handiwork. Day unto day utters speech, and night unto night reveals knowledge. There is no speech nor language where their voice is not heard (Psalm 19:1-3).

The Apostle Paul told the people in Lystra:

You should turn from these vain things to the living God, who made the heaven, the earth, the sea, and all things that are in them, who in bygone generations allowed all nations to walk in their own ways. Nevertheless He did not leave Himself without witness, in that He did good, gave us rain from heaven and fruitful seasons, filling our hearts with food and gladness (Acts 14:15-17).

To the church at Rome the Apostle Paul wrote:

For since the creation of the world His invisible attributes are clearly seen, being understood by the things that are made, even His eternal power and Godhead, so that they are without excuse (Romans 1:20).

These passages are reminders that God's creative work can be observed in nature. He created things to function in an orderly fashion and He continues to keep things in order. His handiwork is present everywhere for all to view. One need only look around.

IS NATURE ENOUGH FOR US TO KNOW GOD?

Can a person know God from observing nature? Is it possible to discover who God is and what He is like by looking at the world around us? The answer is no. Though nature testifies that God does exist, in the final analysis it is only God Himself who can give us knowledge of His own being. The Bible makes it clear that God's revelation of Himself in nature is not sufficient knowledge for sinful man to know Him.

Then Paul stood in the midst of the Areopagus and said, 'Men of Athens, I perceive that in all things you are very religious; for as I was passing through and considering the objects of your worship, I even found an altar with this inscription: TO THE UNKNOWN GOD. Therefore, the One, whom you worship without knowing, Him I proclaim to you' (Act 17:22,23).

Paul wrote to the Ephesians:

To me . . . this grace was given, that I should preach among the Gentiles the unsearchable riches of Christ, and to make all people see what is the fellowship of the mystery, which from the beginning of the ages has been hidden in God who created all things through Jesus Christ (Ephesians 3:8,9).

Need God's Word

Any conclusions about God's character and purpose one might make from nature must be evaluated in light of what God has said about Himself and what Jesus, God Himself, revealed about God when He invaded history.

WHERE DOES GOD LIVE?

Is there a particular place that God lives?

The Bible teaches that God's presence is everywhere in the universe. This does not mean that God's substance is spread out everywhere; it simply means that God knows what is occurring at all places and at all times.

When King Solomon prayed to dedicate the temple at Jerusalem he acknowledged this fact.

> But will God dwell on the earth? Behold, the heaven and the heaven of heavens cannot contain You. How much less this temple which I have built! (1 Kings 8:27).

Yet the Bible also states that there is a particular place where He inhabits. God's dwelling place is known by a number of different names, but the most familiar is heaven.

> Look down from heaven, and see from Your habitation, holy and glorious (Isaiah 63:15).

Another designation is the high and holy place:

> For thus says the High and Lofty One who inhabits eternity, whose name is Holy: 'I dwell in the high and holy place' (Isaiah 57:15).

Heaven is also called the throne of God.

> But I say to you, do not swear at all: neither by heaven, for it is God's throne (Matthew 5:34).

His Father's House

Jesus also called heaven His Father's house. It is the place where believers will dwell:

> In My Father's house are many mansion; if it were not so, I would have told you. I go to prepare a place for you. And if I go and prepare a place for you, I will come again and receive you to Myself; that where I am, there you may be also (John 14:2,3).

We conclude the following about where God lives:

1. Though God's presence is everywhere in the universe, He resides in a place known as heaven.

2. From the references in the Bible, we know that heaven is a real, but not material or geographical, place where God resides, and where believers will eventually go to join Him.

15

CAN A PERSON EXPERIENCE GOD THROUGH RELIGIONS OTHER THAN CHRISTIANITY?

Scripture reveals that the God of the Bible is the one true God. God has revealed Himself to mankind in the Scriptures and made provision for us to know Him.

The Bible also warns us about other religions and other gods.

You shall have no other gods before me (Exodus 20:3).

Made a Way

God has provided a way that individuals may know Him. This is through the person of Jesus Christ.

Most assuredly, I say to you, I am the door of the sheep. All who ever came before Me are thieves and robbers, but the sheep did not hear them. I am the door. If anyone enters by Me, he will be saved, and will go in and out and find pasture (John 10:7-9).

Jesus said . . . I am the way, the truth, and the life. No one comes to the Father except through Me (John 14:6).

The Apostle Peter made it clear that a person could know the true God only through Jesus Christ:

Nor is there salvation in any other, for there is no other name under heaven given among men by which we must be saved (Acts 4:12).

Religions that offer the individual a way to know God other than through the person of Jesus Christ are false religions. As Paul Little wrote:

Christianity is what God has done for man in seeking Him and reaching down to help him. Other religions are a matter of man seeking and struggling toward God . . . Because of this profound difference, Christianity alone offers assurance of salvation (Paul Little, *Know What You Believe*, Intervarsity Press, p. 93).

Thus we conclude:

1. The Bible says there is only one God.

2. God has provided a way by which people may know Him, through the person of Jesus Christ.

3. Jesus said that nobody can come to God except through Him.

4. Any religion, therefore, that teaches God may be reached apart from Jesus is incorrect at that point.

DO OTHER GODS EXIST?

Apart from the God of the Bible could other gods possibly exist? Does the Bible have anything to say about the existence of other gods?

No Other gods

The Bible is clear that although there be other so-called gods, there is only one eternal God who exists.

> You are my witnesses, says the Lord, and my servants whom I have chosen, that you may know and believe Me, and understand that I am He, before Me there was no God formed, nor shall there be after Me (Isaiah 43:10).

Though the Bible makes reference to false gods it does not state that these are actual gods who exist. The Apostle Paul wrote:

> But, then indeed, when you did not know God, you served those which by nature are not gods (Galatians 4:8).

Scripture shows that these false gods are not to be compared with the one, true God.

> To whom will you liken Me, and make Me equal and compare Me, that we should be alike? They lavish gold out of the bag, and weigh silver in the balance; they hire a goldsmith, and he makes it a god; they prostrate themselves, yes, they worship. They bear it on the

shoulder, they carry it and set it in its place, and it stands; from its place it shall not move. Though one cries out to it, yet it cannot answer nor save him out of trouble (Isaiah 46:5-7).

These so-called gods were inventions in the mind of people who rejected the truth of the one true God. Only the God of the Bible has real substance.

Since the God of the Bible has given us reason to believe in His existence whatever He might say on the matter of other gods is final. Because God says He is the only God who exists that solves the question. There are no other true gods.

HOW DO EASTERN RELIGIONS VIEW GOD?

The great religions of the world have a different conception of God than does Christianity. When they are compared, it is obvious that their views of God are incompatible with Christianity.

The Eastern religions make no ultimate distinction between God and his creation. He is the same as the created universe. God is all and all is god. The Bible does not teach this. God is separate from His creation.

In the beginning God created the heavens and the earth (Genesis 1:1).

God existed before the universe as a personal being. When He created the physical universe He brought into existence something that did not exist before.

By faith we understand that the worlds were framed by the word of God, so that the things which are seen were not made of things which are visible (Hebrews 11:3).

This new creation was not an extension of God's being or nature. It is a totally different entity. According to the Bible God is not the same as His creation.

For every house is built by someone, but He who builds all things is God (Hebrews 3:4).

Impersonal Being

Because the Eastern religions view God as one with the universe, he is ultimately impersonal, rather than a being with personality. Christianity teaches that God is personal. "For God so loved the world" (John 3:16).

This verse teaches that God has a capacity to love the world. The god of the Eastern religions cannot love the world because he is the same entity as the world. The God of the Bible can think, love, reason, hate, and judge. The god of the Eastern religions can do none of these things.

No Interest in Man

Also the impersonal god of the Eastern religions cannot have any interest in the affairs of man. Thus there is no one to pray to, no one to look out for man.

The Bible pictures God as intimately involved in man and what he does. Jesus said:

Come to Me, all you who labor and are heavy laden, and I will give you rest (Matthew 11:28).

The God of Christianity, therefore, is not the same God as pictured in the Eastern religions for the following reasons:

1. The god of the Eastern religions is the same as the creation, the God of Christianity is different than His creation.

2. The god of the Eastern religions is impersonal while the God of Christianity is a personal being.

3. The impersonal god of the East cannot have any interest in mankind while the God of Christianity is intimately concerned in the affairs of men.

IS THE GOD OF ISLAM THE SAME GOD AS CHRISTIANITY?

Is Allah, the god of Islam, the same God as the One revealed in the Bible?

The religion of Islam was founded by a man named Mohammed who was born in A.D. 570. Mohammed claimed to receive revelations from God that went beyond the Scriptures of Judaism and Christianity.

But the evidence speaks otherwise. The concept of God in Christianity and Islam is not the same. It is not possible that Muslims and Christians worship the same God. The two religions have a different source of authority, different view of Jesus Christ, and different view of salvation.

Different Source of Authority

According to Islam the final source of authority is the Koran, which Muslims believe to be the word of God. Although Islam teaches that the Old and New Testaments are divinely inspired they believe that Christians and Jews have corrupted the Scriptures. Islam considers the Bible wrong in any place where it conflicts with the Koran. The Koran is the only trustworthy source of teaching for the Muslims.

Different God

The Koran portrays a different god than Christianity. The god of Islam is called Allah and within his nature there is only one person. The Bible teaches that there is one eternal God who has revealed Himself in three eternal persons, the Father, the Son, and the Holy Spirit. These three persons are the one God. This is the doctrine of the Trinity. Islam rejects the Trinity and the New Testament teaching that Jesus Christ is the eternal God. They consider Him only a prophet:

Jesus Christ, the son of Mary, was no more than an apostle of God (Sura 19:92).

This statement is in direct contradiction to what the Bible says about Jesus:

In the beginning was the Word, and the Word was with God, and the Word was God (John 1:1).

Islam believes that its founder Mohammed was the last and greatest of the prophets.

Different Way of Salvation

Finally, Islam teaches a different way by which a person can know God and be saved from their sins. Islam's standard of measurement is a person's good deeds.

They whose balances shall be heavy shall be blest. But they whose balances shall be light, they shall lose their soul, abiding in hell forever (Sura 13:102-104).

The Bible says that our good works cannot please God. We need a Savior. Jesus is the one who died to save us from our sins. We must accept the forgiveness He offers by faith. We cannot earn our salvation.

Not by works of righteousness which we have done, but according to His mercy He saved us (Titus 3:5).

Islam rejects the salvation that is offered by Jesus Christ.

We conclude that the God of Islam and the God of Christianity are not compatible for the following reasons:

1. The sources of authority are different. Islam accepts the Koran as its final authority and believes that the Bible contains errors. The Bible teaches that it is the

inerrant Word of God and final authority on all matters, including faith and practice.

2 Islam believes that Jesus was only a great prophet. The New Testament teaches He is the eternal God. Islam elevates Mohammed to a greater position than Jesus.

3 Islam teaches that a person can be saved by his own good deeds while the Bible teaches that only through belief in Christ can a person be saved. Thus Allah, the God of Islam, is not the God revealed in the Bible.

WHAT IS ATHEISM?

The word atheism comes from the Greek prefix *a* meaning "no or non" and the word *theos* meaning "god or God." An atheist is one who believes that God does not exist. The atheist explains all of existence in a natural rather than supernatural manner. When he looks at the world around him he sees it as a product of natural forces. The atheist considers religious belief in a god or gods as without ultimate meaning.

The atheist believes that proof of the non-existence of God is available. He contends that there is convincing evidence that God does not exist. Yet the atheist himself cannot know with certainty that God or gods do not exist.

Two Possible Ways

This is because there are only two possible ways that anyone could know that God did not exist.

Since it is possible that a god exists somewhere in the universe who has not communicated to us, a person would have to have complete knowledge of everything that is going on in every part of the universe to categorically make the claim that God does not exist. Of course if that person had sufficient knowledge to be able to make the statement that God does not exist, he would be all-knowing and then, by definition, he would be God. Otherwise he could not know with certainty whether or not a god or gods do exist.

Special Revelation

Someone could know that God did not exist if he received a special revelation informing him that there exists no god or gods in the universe. But only God Himself could give that special revelation, so this way of denying God's existence is also ruled out.

Thus to state that God does not exist is to commit the fallacy of categorical denial. One should more properly say, I do not believe that there is evidence of the existence of God rather than saying there is no God. On that basis, the atheist can then present his case as to why he thinks God does not exist and the theist, the one who believes in God, can counter the atheist's arguments of why he believes that God does exist.

20

WHAT IS AGNOSTICISM?

Agnosticism comes from the Greek prefix *a-* "no or non" and the noun *gnosis* "knowledge." An agnostic is a person who believes that there is insufficient evidence to prove or disprove the existence of God or gods. The agnostic criticizes both the theist and atheist for holding their position with such certainty. The agnostic tries to maintain a neutralist position.

Two Types of Agnostics

There are basically two types of agnostics. One type says that there is insufficient evidence that God exists but leaves open the possibility of attaining that evidence at some future time. This type of agnostic considers it possible to have enough evidence to know with certainty that God exists.

There is another type of agnostic who believes it is impossible for anyone to ever know with certainty whether or not God or gods exist. This group feels that the facts are not now available and never will be available to make such a decision.

Christian theologians Norman Geisler and Paul Feinberg expand on the distinction between the two types of agnostics:

> One form of agnosticism claims that we *do not* know if God exists; the other insists that we *cannot* know. The first we'll call "soft" and the second "hard" agnosticism. . . [Soft agnosticism] does not eliminate in principle the

possibility of knowing whether God exists. It says in effect, "I do not know whether God exists but it is not impossible to know. I simply do not have enough evidence to make a rational decision on the question" . . . [Hard agnosticism] claims that it is impossible to know whether God exists (Norman Geisler and Paul Feinberg, *Introduction to Philosophy: A Christian Perspective*, Grand Rapids, MI: Baker Book House, 1980, p. 26).

We can, therefore, break down the categories of agnostics into two groups. Those that say we do not know whether or not God exists and those that say we cannot know whether or not God exists.

Biblical Answer

The Apostle Paul encountered agnostics in his day. The Bible records how Paul dealt with this group in a sermon he gave in Athens:

Then Paul stood in the midst of the Areopagus and said, "Men of Athens, I perceive in all things you are very religious; for as I was passing through and considering the objects of your worship, I even found an altar with this inscription: TO THE UNKNOWN GOD. Therefore, the One whom you worship, without knowing, Him I proclaim to you: God who made the world and everything in it, since He is Lord of heaven and earth, does not dwell in temples made with hands. Nor is He worshiped with men's hands, as though He needed anything, since He gives to all life, breath, and all things. And He has made from one blood every nation of men to dwell on all the face of the earth, and has determined their preappointed times and the boundaries of their habitation, so that they should seek the Lord, in the hope that they might grope for Him and find Him, though He is not far from each one of us (Acts 17:22-27).

The message of Scripture is loud and clear. God exists, and it is possible to have knowledge of that fact as well as a personal relationship with Him.

CONCLUSION TO PART 1

After investigating the evidence of God's existence we have come to the following conclusions:

1. The Bible teaches the existence of God.

2. God has always existed. Nobody created Him.

3. There is only one God who exists. There are no other gods.

4. The one God has eternally existed in three persons, the Father, the Son, and the Holy Spirit. This is known as the doctrine of the Trinity.

5. God has given mankind sufficient reason to believe that He exists. Some of the reasons we know that God exists include: the Bible, predictive prophecy, the resurrection of Jesus Christ, and the changed lives of believers.

Since there is sufficient evidence that God exists the next logical question concerns what He is like? What are the characteristics of God? What can He do? Is there anything He is not capable of doing? Part 2, The Nature of God, will address these and other related questions.

PART 2

GOD: HIS NATURE

Oh, the depth of the riches both of the wisdom
and knowledge of God! How unsearchable are His
judgments and His ways past finding out!
—Romans 11:33

IS EVERYTHING THAT EXISTS PART OF GOD?

There is a view of God's nature known as pantheism. The term is derived from two Greek words *pan* and *theos*. *Pan* means "all or everything" and *theos* means "God." Pantheism, therefore, means god is everything.

Pantheism teaches that everything that exists is part of one single reality and that reality is called god. God is all and all is god. There is no distinction between the creature and the creator in pantheism. God is equal to anything and everything. The concept of a personal God who created the universe as a separate substance is foreign to pantheism.

God is Separate

However, the Scripture states otherwise:

In the beginning God created the heavens and the earth (Genesis 1:1).

For since the creation of the world His invisible attributes are clearly seen, being understood by the things that are made, even His eternal power and Godhead (Romans 1:20).

The universe has not existed eternally but God has. When God created the universe He brought into being something different from Himself.

By faith we understand that the worlds were framed by the word of God, so that the things which are seen were not made of things which are visible (Hebrews 11:3).

Pantheism blurs this distinction. The God of the Bible is not the same God of pantheism.

IS GOD A PERSONAL GOD?

The God who is revealed in the Bible is a personal God. This means that He has the characteristics of a person. A person can be defined as someone who is rational, conscious of his own being. This is how the Bible portrays God. He is a person, not an impersonal force. The Bible speaks of Him as the living God:

But the Lord is the true God; He is the living God and the everlasting King (Jeremiah 10:10).

The Scriptures attribute characteristics to God that can only be those of a person.

Love

The Bible speaks of God having the capacity to love.

The Lord has appeared of old to me, saying: 'Yes I have loved you with an everlasting love' (Jeremiah 31:3).

But God demonstrates His own love toward us, in that while we were still sinners, Christ died for us (Romans 5:8).

Anger

God also can show anger.

And the Lord said to Moses . . . 'Now therefore, let Me alone, that My wrath may burn hot against them and I may consume them' (Exodus 32:10,11).

Mercy

The Scriptures teach that God has the ability to show mercy.

Then God saw their works, that they turned from their evil way; and God relented from the disaster that He had said He would bring upon them, and He did not do it (Jonah 3:10).

The Bible speaks of God as wanting or desiring things.

The Lord is not slack concerning His promise, as some count slackness, but is longsuffering toward us, not willing that any should perish but that all should come to repentance (2 Peter 3:9).

Intellect

The Bible says that God has an intellect. He has a mind that thinks. God uses His mind to instruct His people concerning what they should do.

Thus says the Lord, your Redeemer, the Holy One of Israel: 'I am the Lord your God who teaches you to profit, who leads you by the way you should go' (Isaiah 48:17).

These are some of the attributes that the Bible says God possesses. They are all consistent with personhood. By demonstrating these in His character God has shown that He is a personal God.

Contrasted with Idols

The Bible also contrasts the personal living God to idols, which neither hear nor speak. The Apostle Paul told a crowd at Lystra:

Men, why are you doing these things? We also are men with the same nature as you, and preach to you that you should turn from these vain things to the living God, who made the heaven, the earth, the sea, and all things in them (Acts 14:15).

When he wrote to the church at Thessalonica Paul again brought out the distinction between the living God and non-living idols.

For they themselves declare concerning us what manner of entry we had to you, and how you turned to God from idols to serve the living and true God (1 Thessalonians 1:9).

Hence the Bible contrasts the living God who hears, sees, thinks, feels, and acts like a person with idols which are things, not persons.

We sum up as follows:

1. The Bible designates God as the living God. He is a rational being, conscious of His existence.

2. As the living God He possesses the attributes of a person. For, among other things, He can love, express anger, and show mercy. The Bible also says that God has a will and an intellect. All of these characteristics are consistent with personhood.

3. Furthermore, the Bible contrasts the personal living God with impersonal idols which are mere things.

We conclude the Bible clearly teaches that God is personal.

IS GOD GOOD?

One of the characteristics of God is His goodness. The Bible makes it clear that God is good. Jesus said:

No one is good but One, that is, God (Mark 10:18).

What is meant by this? In what ways is God good?

God Watches Over His Creation

God demonstrates His goodness to us in a variety of ways. One way is that He grants mercy to His creation. This is known as common grace. This common grace extends to believer and unbeliever alike. Jesus said:

He makes His sun rise on the evil and on the good, and sends rain on the just and on the unjust (Matthew 5:45).

Provides What is Necessary

The Apostle Paul stated that God provides for His creation the things necessary for existence.

Nevertheless He did not leave Himself without witness, in that He did good, gave us rain from heaven and fruitful seasons, filling our hearts with food and gladness (Acts 14:17).

Gives Good Things to Believers

God also grants His goodness to the particular individuals who believe in Him.

Whoever believes in Him should not perish but have everlasting life (John 3:16).

His goodness is not only demonstrated by the granting of salvation to all who believe, but the loving care in watching over His people:

The Lord, the Lord God, merciful and gracious, longsuffering, and abounding in goodness and truth, keeping mercy for thousands, forgiving iniquity and transgression and sin (Exodus 34:6,7).

Now if God so clothes the grass of the field, which today is, and tomorrow is thrown into the oven, will He not much more clothe you, O you of little faith (Matthew 6:30).

God is Patient

God's goodness is also exhibited in His patience. He waits for people to come to Him by faith by giving them time to repent of their sins:

The Lord is not slack concerning His promise, as some count slackness, but is longsuffering toward us, not willing that any should perish but that all should come to repentance (2 Peter 3:9).

Or do you despise the riches of His goodness, forbearance, and longsuffering, not knowing the goodness of God leads to repentance (Romans 2:4).

God's goodness is demonstrated to us in the following ways.

1. He provides for all mankind by keeping the universe running in an orderly fashion.

2. He gives special privileges to those who put their faith in Him.

3. God is patient with the unbeliever giving him many chances to repent of his sins.

CAN ANYTHING ABOUT GOD CHANGE?

Is it possible that God can change in His promises or in His character? Can the laws that God has set down be changed? Can we be assured that God will never change?

When one changes he usually changes for better or worse. Since God is absolute perfection no change for the better is possible since you cannot improve upon perfection. The same holds true for changing for the worst. Change is not possible with God.

The Scripture makes it clear that God does not change in His character, His fairness toward mankind, or in His promises.

God's Character is Unchanged

The Bible insists that the basic character of God is not subject to change. The psalmist said of God:

You are the same, and Your years will have no end (Psalm 102:27).

In the Book of Malachi God declares:

For I am the Lord, I do not change (Malachi 3:6).

The New Testament also says God does not change:

Every good gift and every perfect gift is from above, and comes down from the Father of lights, with whom there is no variation or shadow of turning (James 1:17).

Nature

God, by nature, is a Trinity consisting of the Father, the Son, and the Holy Spirit. He has always been a Trinity and He always will be. His basic nature will remain forever the same.

Because God's nature does not change His character remains the same. He has been and always will be completely righteous. This means His dealings with mankind are always right; He is never unfair.

The Apostle Paul said of God:

Because He has appointed a day on which He will judge the world in righteousness by the Man whom He has ordained (Acts 17:31).

God will judge mankind based upon the standard that He has set down. God will not change those standards. His judgment will be fair.

His Promises

The Bible also testifies that God does not change in His promises. The Lord said of Himself.

God is not a man, that He should lie, nor a son of man, that He should repent (Numbers 23:19).

The Bible emphasizes that God is faithful to the promises which He has made to mankind. The prophet Jeremiah said:

Through the Lord's mercies we are not consumed, because His compassions fail not, they are new every morning; great is Your faithfulness (Lamentations 3:22,23).

When God promises something to us He will complete His promise. Some of the promises God has made to man are conditional, based upon man's response. The prophet Jeremiah records God saying:

The instant I speak concerning a nation and concerning a kingdom, to pluck up, to pull down, and to

destroy it, if that nation against whom I have spoken
turns from its evil, I will relent of the disaster that I
thought to bring upon it. And the instant I speak
concerning a nation and concerning a kingdom, to build
and to plant it, if it does evil in My sight so that it does not
obey My voice, then I will relent concerning the good
which I said I would benefit from it (Jeremiah 18:7-10).

Therefore we conclude from the Bible that God will
never change in His:

1. Basic character.

2. Fairness toward mankind.

3. Promises.

We can rest assured that God will remain the same.
But when we say God does not change we do not mean
that He is a static, impersonal being. God dynamically
interacts with His creation. It is God's character and
promises that do not change.

WHY DOES THE BIBLE SAY GOD CHANGED HIS MIND?

If we accept the fact that God is perfection and that He cannot change how do we account for certain parts of the Bible that seem to indicate that God changed His mind? There are several instances in the Scripture where God relents, or changes His mind, about something that He was going to do.

When Moses came down from Mt. Sinai after receiving the ten commandments (Exodus 32) he found that the people had fallen into sin. They had made for themselves a golden calf and were worshipping it. God then told Moses that He was ready to destroy the nation. Moses pleaded for the people and the Scripture says,

> So the Lord relented of the harm which He said He would do to His people (Exodus 32:14).

Is this not an example of God changing His mind?

In the Book of Jonah we have a similar situation. God was going to destroy the people of Nineveh. They repented of their sins and God had mercy on them.

> Then God saw their works, that they turned from their evil way; and God relented from the disaster that He had said He would bring upon them, and He did not do it (Jonah 3:10).

From Man's Viewpoint

The seeming changing of God's mind in these and in other situations makes people wonder if God is wavering in His word. But this is not the case. In the situation with Moses God was angry because the people had rejected Him in favor of an idol. His desire to destroy them was not unalterable. Moses' intercession on behalf of the people kept them from being destroyed. From man's point of view God's mind was changed but God had known all along what would happen. Moses prayed for mercy and God answered his prayer.

The same is true in the case of Jonah and Nineveh. The people of Nineveh prayed to God and asked His forgiveness. God heard their prayer and granted mercy to them. He did not change His mind for He knew all along they would repent of their sins. Yet from man's point of view this was unknown. The people had not been assured that God would stop judgment if they repented but Jonah had an idea that this might happen. When the prophet realized that Nineveh would not be destroyed he prayed to God and said:

Ah, Lord, was not this what I said when I was still in my country? Therefore I fled previously to Tarshish; for I know that You are a gracious and merciful God, slow to anger and abundant in lovingkindness, One who relents from doing harm (Jonah 4:2).

Change Was With Man

We see in both these instances that a prayer of repentance changed the outcome of the situation. The change was not with God but with man. When the conduct of man changed towards God, the conduct of God changed toward man.

When Scripture tells us about God relenting, or repenting, of what He said He would do, each instance is in regard to punishment. It is never a case of God promising to do something good and then changing His mind. His promises to His people will not be broken.

For the gifts and calling of God are irrevocable (Romans 8:29).

Thus the Bible assures us of the following:

1. God will not change toward us with His promises.

2. Any seeming change in God's dealings is from man's point of view not God's.

3. Every time God changed His mind it was in favor of man rather than against him.

DOES GOD KNOW EVERYTHING?

The Bible teaches that God is all-knowing or omniscient. That means that He has perfect knowledge of all things. He does not have to learn anything and He has not forgotten anything. He knows everything that has happened and everything that will happen. God also knows every potential thing that might happen. The psalmist wrote:

Great is our Lord, and mighty in power; His understanding is infinite (Psalm 147:5).

John the evangelist wrote:

For if our heart condemn us, God is greater than our heart, and knows all things (1 John 3:20).

In the Book of Job a man named Elihu said:

Do you know the balance of the clouds, those wondrous works of Him who is perfect in knowledge (Job 37:16).

The Bible says that God knows every star in the universe.

He counts the number of the stars; He calls them all by name (Psalm 147:4).

Smallest Details

Jesus taught that God is also concerned with everything down to the smallest of details:

Are not two sparrows sold for a copper coin? And not one of them falls to the ground apart from your Father's will. But the very hairs of your head are all numbered (Matthew 10:29,30).

God has had all knowledge for all eternity:

Known to God from eternity are all His works (Acts 15:18).

We conclude that the Bible clearly teaches that God's knowledge is without limit. The Apostle Paul declared:

Oh, the depth of the riches both of the wisdom and knowledge of God! How unsearchable are His judgments and His ways past finding out (Romans 11:33).

IS GOD EVERYWHERE AT ONCE?

The Bible teaches that God is everywhere present—omnipresent. In every place in the universe God is present. The psalmist wrote:

Where can I go from your Spirit? Or where can I flee from Your presence? If I ascend into heaven, You are there; if I make my bed in hell, behold, You are there; if I take the wings of the morning and dwell in the uttermost parts of the sea, even there Your hand shall lead me, and Your right hand shall hold me (Psalm 137:7-10).

Nobody can Hide

The prophet Amos records God as saying that no one can hide from Him:

Though they dig into hell, from there my hand shall take them; though they climb up to heaven, from there I will bring them down; and though they hide themselves on top of Carmel, from there I will search and take them; though they hide from My sight at the bottom of the sea, from there I will command the serpent, and it shall bite them (Amos 9:2,3).

In the Book of Jeremiah God says:

'Am I a God near at hand,' says the Lord, 'and not a God afar off? Can anyone hide himself in secret places, so

I shall not see him?' . . . 'do I not fill heaven and earth?'
says the Lord? (Jeremiah 23:23,24).

The Bible is clear that there is no place in the universe
that is away from God's presence. His presence is
everywhere.

This is not to say that God's form is spread out so that
parts of Him exist in every location. God is spirit, He has no
physical form. He is present everywhere in that everything
is immediately in His presence. No one can hide from Him
and nothing escapes His notice.

IS GOD
ALL-POWERFUL?

When the Bible speaks of God it speaks of Him as being all-powerful—omnipotent. He appeared to Abraham as the Almighty God.

I am Almighty God; walk before Me and be blameless (Genesis 17:1).

Nothing too Difficult

God said that nothing was too difficult for Him to do. Anything that can be done, God can do.

Behold, I am the Lord, the God of all flesh. Is there anything too hard for Me? (Jeremiah 32:27).

The psalmist testified of His power:

Come and see the works of God; He is awesome in His doing toward the sons of men. He turned the sea into dry land; they went through the river on foot . . . He rules by His power forever; His eyes observe the nations; do not let the rebellious exalt themselves (Psalm 66:5-7).

But does this mean He can do anything? Can God destroy Himself? Can He make a being that He cannot control? No, God cannot do what is logically or actually impossible. He cannot contradict His nature or character. That is not within the realm of His power.

Limits

There are limits to what God can do. For example the Bible says that God cannot lie:

In hope of eternal life which God, who cannot lie, promised before time began (Titus 1:2).

God has also stated that He cannot go back on His Word:

Forever, O Lord, Your word is settled in heaven (Psalm 119:89).

Since there are certain things that God cannot do how can He be all-powerful?

Proper Understanding Needed

The answer lies in a proper understanding of God's omnipotence. Omnipotence does not mean God cannot exercise self-limitation. The biblical God has limited Himself only to acts that are consistent with His righteous, loving character. Therefore, God's power, is self-restrained. He cannot do evil and He cannot do anything irrational. He cannot go back upon His word. He is all-powerful when it comes to doing things that are right but He has no power to do things wrong.

IS GOD LOVE?

The Bible makes it clear that one of the characteristics of God's nature is that He is love.

> He who does not love does not know God, for God is love (1 John 4:8).

Seeking Highest Good

Love may be defined as seeking the highest good of another. God has clearly demonstrated His love for mankind:

> In this the love of God was manifested toward us, that God has sent His only begotten Son into the world, that we might live through Him (1 John 4:9).

> But God demonstrates His own love toward us, in that while we were still sinners, Christ died for us (Romans 5:8).

God has shown His love for the world when He sent Christ to die for our sins. In like manner we are to imitate Christ by selflessly giving ourselves to the needs of others. Jesus said:

> A new commandment I give to you, that you love one another; as I have loved you, that you also love one another (John 13:34).

The Apostle Paul echoed this thought:

> Let each of you look out not only for his own interests, but also for the interests of others (Philippians 2:4).

One of God's most obvious attributes is love. Yet it must be understood that He is not equivalent to love. Love is an attribute of God. We can rightly say that God is love but we cannot say that love is God for that would make God impersonal.

IS GOD RIGHTEOUS?

The Bible speaks of God being righteous.

O Lord God of Israel, You are righteous (Ezra 9:15).

Gracious is the Lord and righteous; yes, our God is merciful (Psalm 116:5).

What does the Bible mean when it says that God is righteous? This means that God's character or nature always leads Him to do that which is right. We can also refer to God's righteousness as God's justice. The Bible says:

The Lord is righteous, He is in her midst, He will do no unrighteousness. Every morning He brings His justice to light; He never fails, but the unjust knows no shame (Zephaniah 3:5).

Love Good and Hate Evil

God reveals His righteousness by loving the things that are good and by hating the things that are evil. Consequently His righteousness sometimes results in judgment:

And I heard the angel of the waters saying: 'You are righteous, O Lord, the One who is and who was and who is to be, because You have judged these things' (Revelation 16:5).

Then hear in heaven, and act and judge Your servants, condemning the wicked, bringing his way on his head, and justifying the righteous by giving him according to his righteousness (1 Kings 8:32).

God promises, however, to reward those who have been faithful to Him.

Oh let the wickedness of the wicked come to an end, but establish the just; for the righteous God tests the hearts and minds. My defense is of God who saves the upright in heart. God is a just judge, and God is angry with the wicked every day (Psalm 7:9-11).

Finally, there is laid up for me the crown of righteousness, which the Lord, the righteous Judge, will give me on that Day, and not to me only but also to all who love His appearing (2 Timothy 4:8).

Therefore we can conclude the following about the righteousness of God:

1. God's righteousness, or justice, is an attribute that leads Him to do only those things which are right.

2. Because God is righteous He must judge evil.

3. God's justice allows Him to reward those who have been faithful to Him.

31

WHAT DOES IT MEAN: GOD IS HOLY?

The Bible teaches that God is a holy God. The idea behind the concept of holiness is separation. God is separate from everything that is sinful and evil. He cannot tolerate sin. Because He is holy He can only do that which is true and good.

Word is True

God's word is truth. Jesus said:

Sanctify them by Your truth. Your word is truth (John 17:17).

God has promised that He will not go back on His word:

In hope of eternal life which God, who cannot lie, promised before time began (Titus 1:2).

God's revealed Word, the Bible, tells us that He is perfect in all that He is. There is nothing morally lacking in His character. God is perfection.

What About Judgment?

This brings up the matter of judgment. Because He is holy and cannot tolerate sin there must be some way to judge wrongdoing. His holiness demands justice for sins that are committed. It was our sin that separated us from the holiness of God. God's word says:

But your iniquities have separated you from your God; and your sins have hidden His face from you (Isaiah 59:2).

This is the reason God placed the penalty of the sins of the world upon Jesus when He was crucified on our behalf.

For He made Him who knew no sin to be sin for us, that we might become the righteousness of God in Him (2 Corinthians 5:21).

His holiness has been satisfied with the death of Christ. We can now enter into God's presence based upon the sacrifice Christ made on the cross.
Once that relationship has been restored we are told:

You shall be holy, for I the Lord your God am holy (Leviticus 19:2).

In conclusion we can say concerning the holiness of God:

1. The main idea behind holiness is separation.

2. God is separate from sin. He is perfect in His nature.

3. His perfection demands justice for sin. Christ died on the cross to satisfy the holy demands of God.

WHAT IS THE GLORY OF GOD?

The Bible speaks of the glory of God.

> In the morning you shall see the glory of the Lord . . . Now it came to pass, as Aaron spoke to the whole of the congregation of the children of Israel, and they looked toward the wilderness, and behold the glory of the Lord appeared in a cloud (Exodus 16:7,10).

What is the glory of God? God's glory is His splendor, His majesty. The Bible uses God's glory figuratively as a manifestation of Himself. The Bible attributes many appearances and actions of God with His glory.

When Moses went up on Mt. Sinai to receive the ten commandments from God, the glory of the Lord rested upon the mountain.

> Then Moses went up into the mountain, and a cloud covered the mountain. Now the glory of the Lord rested on Mt. Sinai, and the cloud covered it six days. And on the seventh day He called to Moses out of the midst of the cloud. The sight of the glory of the Lord was like a consuming fire on top of the mountain in the eyes of the children of Israel (Exodus 24:15-17).

When the people disobeyed God His glory departed from them.

The glory of the Lord has departed from Israel because the ark of God has been captured (1 Samuel 4:21).

Used Figuratively for God

The glory of God is used figuratively for God Himself. Moses said to God:

Please show me Your glory. Then He said, I will make all my goodness pass before you, and I will proclaim the name of the Lord before you. . . You cannot see My face; for no man shall see Me and live. And the Lord said, here is a place by Me, and you shall stand on the rock. So shall it be, while My glory passes by, that I will put you in the cleft of the rock, and will cover you with My hand while I pass by (Exodus 33:18-22).

We conclude about the glory of God.

1   God's glory is His splendor, His majesty.

2   Sometimes God's glory is used figuratively of Himself.

WHAT'S THE DIFFERENCE BETWEEN MAN AND GOD?

The Bible says that there is a great gulf between the creature and the Creator.

Creator and Created

First we need to understand that God is the Creator while man is His creation. We are His work. He was created by no one. The Bible speaks of God existing in the beginning.

In the beginning was the Word, and the Word was with God, and the Word was God (John 1:1).

Man is the creation.

So God created man in His own image; in the image of God He created him; male and female He created them (Genesis 1:27).

Finite and Infinite

Also God is eternal. He always has existed and always will exist.

Before the mountains were brought forth, or even You had formed the earth and the world, even from everlasting to everlasting, You are God (Psalm 90:2).

Man, on the other hand, is finite. There was a point in time when he did not exist.

And the Lord God formed man of the dust of the ground, and breathed into his nostrils the breath of life; and man became a living being (Genesis 2:7).

Self-Existent

God alone is self-existent. That is He needs nothing apart from Himself to exist. The Apostle Paul spoke of God's self-existence:

Nor is He worshiped with men's hands, as though He needed anything, since He gives to all life, breath, and all things (Acts 17:25).

But then, indeed, when you did not know God, you served those which by nature are not gods (Galatians 4:8).

He alone is self-existent. He is by nature God. Man has to depend upon many things to exist. The prophet Daniel told king Belshazzar:

And the God who holds your breath in His hand and owns all your ways, you have not glorified (Daniel 5:23).

We can sum up the differences between man and God as follows:

1. God is the Creator, while man is the creation.

2 God is infinite while man is finite.

3 God needs nothing to exist while man has to depend upon something other than himself to exist.

CAN MAN BECOME GOD?

From time to time throughout our history there have been those who claim that man is God or that man can become God. The Mormon church, for example, teaches that Mormons have the power to attain godhood. Does the Bible teach that man can become God?

The false promise that man can become God goes as far back as the first man, Adam. When Adam and Eve were in the Garden of Eden the only negative commandment God gave them was not to eat of fruit of the tree of the knowledge of good and evil. The serpent appeared to them and disputed God:

> For God knows that in the day you eat of it your eyes will be opened, and you will be like God, knowing good and evil (Genesis 3:5).

When they ate of the fruit they did not become as God as the serpent promised. Rather they brought sin into the world and were banished from God's presence. Satan, however, has been telling people that lie ever since. And, unfortunately, people still believe it.

Nature of God

The reason man cannot become God is because of the nature of God. God did not become God at some certain point. He has been, is, and always will be God. He is the eternal infinite God. There is nothing lacking in His character and He needs nothing to exist. He is adequate in and by Himself.

Moreover He is the only God who now exists or ever will exist:

> Thus says the Lord, the King of Israel, and His Redeemer, the Lord of hosts; I am the First and I am the Last; besides Me there is no God (Isaiah 44:6).

> You are My witnesses, says the Lord, and My servant whom I have chosen, that you may know and believe Me, and understand that I am He. Before Me there was no God formed, nor shall there be after Me (Isaiah 43:10).

Man is Finite

Man, on the other hand, is a finite limited creature. There was a time when he did not exist. When he came into being it was because of the will of God. Man cannot exist by himself. He is not self-sustaining. He needs food, air, water, to stay alive. Without these and other things man would perish.

The Bible says that God will grant everlasting life to those who believe in His Son, Jesus Christ. But this will not mean man will become God. Each individual must depend upon God for everlasting life. Those who promise that man can become God either do not understand the differences between the creature and the Creator or are deliberately perverting the truth of God.

CAN GOD BECOME MAN?

Though it is not possible for man to become God what about the possibility of God becoming a man? Some three thousand years ago there lived a man named Job who was going through much suffering. Job did not think that God understood his pain. Job then cried out for a mediator between God and man.

> Nor He [God] is not a man, as I am, that I may answer Him, and that we should go to court together. Nor is there any mediator between us, who may lay His hand on both of us (Job 9:32,33).

Job's Wish Fulfilled

Job's desire was for God to become a man so that He could personally experience the suffering and limitation that mankind endures. This desire expressed by Job was fulfilled. The New Testament records that two thousand years ago the eternal God became a man in the person of Jesus Christ. When Jesus became a man He did not quit being God and God did not change. The Gospel according to John testifies:

> In the beginning was the Word, and the Word was with God, and the Word was God . . . And the Word became flesh and dwelt among us, and we beheld His glory, the glory as of the only begotten of the Father, full of grace and truth (John 1:1,14).

Jesus suffered the limitation and humiliation of becoming a man on our behalf.

Let this mind be in you which was also in Christ Jesus, who, being in the form of God, did not consider it robbery to be equal with God, but made Himself of no reputation, taking the form of a servant, and coming in the likeness of men (Philippians 2:5-7).

Jesus' coming to earth was for the purpose of revealing God to man and to be that mediator that Job desired. The Apostle Paul records.

For there is one God and One Mediator between God and men, the Man Christ Jesus (1 Timothy 2:5).

God did indeed answer Job's cry. For a short period of time God the Son limited Himself to a body in order to save all of mankind. Because He became like one of us, He is able to personally identify with the suffering and pain that we ourselves experience.

For in that He Himself has suffered, being tempted, He is able to aid those who are tempted (Hebrews 2:18).

The Bible teaches that God made the supreme sacrifice on our behalf. The Creator became like one of His creation for the purpose of making right the relationship that man had broken.

DID GOD EVER TAKE A
PHYSICAL FORM BEFORE
THE COMING OF CHRIST?

The Bible says that God became a man in the person of Jesus Christ:

> And the Word became flesh and dwelt among us (John 1:14).

This is the only time God became flesh and lived with man. Previously God had assumed a temporary physical form. There are eight recorded appearances in the Old Testament where God took upon Himself a physical form for a short duration. Three times He appeared as a man, once in a burning bush that was not consumed, and four times as the Angel of the Lord. Each time that this occurred God intervened in an extraordinary situation.

To Hagar (Genesis 16:9-13)

Hagar was Abraham's mistress, the mother of his son Ishmael. Hagar and Ishmael were banished from Abraham into the desert. As they were dying of thirst the Angel of the Lord appeared to Hagar to provide water for the survival of her and her young child. The Angel of the Lord that appeared to Hagar was God Himself:

Then she called the name of the Lord who spoke to her, You-Are-The-God-Who-Sees; for she said, 'Have I also here seen Him who sees me?' (Genesis 16:13).

God had a plan for Ishmael and his descendants. Therefore, He personally appeared to spare Ishmael.

To Abraham and Sarah at Mamre (Genesis 18:1-33)

Three men appeared to Abraham and his wife Sarah at the plains of Mamre. They had come to inform Abraham and Sarah concerning two matters. The son that God had promised them would be born to Abraham and Sarah the next year, and the evil cities of Sodom and Gomorrah would be destroyed. One of the three visitors who gave them this information is designated as the Lord:

Then the Lord appeared to him by the terebinth trees of Mamre, as he was sitting in the tent door in the heat of the day (Genesis 18:1).

In this same passage this person is called the "Judge of all the earth" (Genesis 18:25). This is a title that belongs to God alone.

To Abraham on Mount Moriah (Genesis 22:11-14)

God told Abraham to bring his son Isaac to Mount Moriah to be sacrificed. Abraham obeyed and was about to take Isaac's life when God intervened. The Angel of the Lord stopped Abraham saying:

Do not lay your hand on the lad, or do anything to him; for now I know that you fear God, seeing that you have not withheld your son, your only son, from Me (Genesis 22:12).

He called a second time to Abraham:

By Myself I have sworn says the Lord (Genesis 22:15).

In this instance the Angel of the Lord, who called out to Abraham, was God.

To Jacob at Peniel (Genesis 32:24-43)

This account has the patriarch Jacob wrestling all night with a man who finally disabled him. The next morning Jacob realized that it was God Himself whom he had wrestled:

> And Jacob called the name of the place Peniel: for I have seen God face to face, and my life is preserved (Genesis 32:30).

To Moses in the Burning Bush (Exodus 3:2-4:17)

When Moses received his call from the Lord to lead the children of Israel out of Egyptian bondage he saw a bush that was burning but not being consumed. A voice came from the bush identifying God's presence:

> God called to him from the midst of the bush and said . . . I am the God of your father—the God of Abraham, the God of Isaac, and the God of Jacob (Exodus 3:4,6).

Because of the magnitude of the task Moses was about to undertake, God personally appeared to him by means of the burning bush.

Gideon (Judges 6:11-24)

Gideon was a man who was called by God to raise an army to defeat the innumerable Midianites. Because Gideon was a timid person God paid him a visit to assure him that all would go well. After the encounter Gideon realized who had visited him:

> Now Gideon perceived that He was the Angel of the Lord. So Gideon said, 'Alas, O Lord God! For I have seen the Angel of the Lord face to face' (Judges 6:22).

Samson's Parents (Judges 13:2-23)

The angel of the Lord appeared to a Jewish woman to announce the birth of a son who would deliver the people of Israel. Because of the importance of the mission God personally appeared to her.

> When the Angel of the Lord appeared no more to Manoah and his wife, then Manoah knew that He was the

Angel of the Lord. And Manoah said to his wife, We shall surely die, because we have seen God (Judges 13:21,22).

Fiery Furnace (Daniel 3:23-29)

The last recorded Old Testament appearance of God in a physical form was to the three young Hebrews in the fiery furnace. Nebuchadnezzar threw the three young men into the furnace because they refused to worship his golden image. God miraculously spared their lives. Nebuchadnezzar was astonished.

Look! he answered, I see four men loose, walking in the midst of the fire; and they are not hurt, and the form of the fourth is like the Son of God (Daniel 3:25).

These eight brief appearances of God in a physical form teach us several things:

1. When an extraordinary situation occurs God is willing to personally appear.

2. These occurrences set a precedent. Since God appeared on these occasions for a short duration during the Old Testament period it set the stage for Him coming in the person of Jesus Christ to live upon the earth.

DOES GOD
HAVE A BODY?

One of the things that many people wonder about God is His form. Does He have a physical or material body? What does God look like?

There are those who reason that since man is made in the image of God and he has a body, then God must also have a body. This assumes that the image of God is physical. But the Bible teaches that God does not have a body.

The Scriptures teach that God is Spirit. Jesus said: "God is Spirit" (John 4:24).

However a person defines spirit, the definition does not include flesh and bones. This can be seen in an encounter Jesus had with His disciples after His resurrection:

> Behold My hands and My feet, that it is I Myself. Handle Me and see, for a spirit does not have flesh and bones as you see I have (Luke 24:39).

Jesus clearly said a spirit does not have flesh and bones. God, therefore, being a spirit, does not have physical form.

God Became a Man

When Jesus came to earth two thousand years ago He took upon Himself a human nature which included a body. Though He will forever be in that body His Divine nature is not material. His body is a human body, not a divine body.

Previously to His coming to earth, He did not possess a body.

We may conclude the following:

1. The Bible teaches God is Spirit.

2. A spirit does not consist of flesh and bones.

3. God, therefore, has no physical form.

4. Jesus took upon Himself human nature including a physical form when He came to the earth, but did not possess a divine body.

WHY DO CERTAIN PASSAGES SEEM TO TEACH THAT GOD HAS A BODY?

We have seen that God is defined as spirit and a spirit does not have a physical form. But there are passages in the Bible that seem to indicate that God does possess a body.

> For the eyes of the Lord run to and fro throughout the whole earth, to show Himself strong on behalf of those whose heart is loyal to Him (2 Chronicles 16:9).

> And remember that you were a slave in the land of Egypt, and that the Lord your God brought you out from there with a mighty hand and by an outstretched arm (Deuteronomy 5:15).

These verses are not to be taken literally. They are to be understood as metaphors that describe in finite human terms, the characteristics of the infinite God. Mankind can better understand and identify with God when He is described as having an outstretched arm, eyes that see everywhere, a mighty hand.

If one wishes to take these references to God's character literally then he will wind up with a very interesting-looking being. Consider these verses:

He shall cover you with His feathers, and under His wings you shall trust (Psalm 91:4).

He had in His right hand seven stars, out of His mouth went a sharp two-edged sword (Revelation 1:16).

Jesus said: "I am the door" (John 10:9).

The writer to the Hebrews stated:

For our God is a consuming fire (Hebrews 12:29).

By taking these verses literally God would look like a bird, have a sword for a tongue, would be made of wood, and would function as a furnace!

Scriptures that seemingly teach that God has a body are not to be understood literally but rather are metaphors to help us better understand the character of God.

DOESN'T THE BIBLE SAY PEOPLE ACTUALLY SAW GOD?

There are several passages of Scripture that seem to indicate people actually saw God:

And Jacob called the name of the place Peniel: for I have seen God face to face, and my life is preserved (Genesis 32:30).

And Moses hid his face, for he was afraid to look upon God (Exodus 3:6).

So the Lord spoke to Moses face to face, as a man speaks to his friend (Exodus 33:11).

But since there has not arisen in Israel a prophet like Moses, whom the Lord knew face to face (Deuteronomy 34:10).

In the year that King Uzziah died, I saw the Lord, sitting on a throne, high and lifted up, and the train of His robe filled the temple (Isaiah 6:1).

Did these people actually see God?

No. What these people saw was not the essence of God but a physical representation of Him. As spirit God is invisible to man. The Apostle Paul said of Jesus:

He is the image of the invisible God (Colossians 1:15).

Though God, in His essence, is invisible He has taken a physical form on occasions to communicate with His creation. He did this for the benefit of those to whom He was speaking. The physical form gave man a point of reference to which he could communicate with God.

But that which the people saw was not the essence of God, for no one has seen or can see God in His essence:

No one has seen God at any time, The only begotten Son, who is in the bosom of the Father, He has declared Him (John 1:18).

Who alone has immortality, dwelling in unapproachable light, whom no man has seen or can see (1 Timothy 6:16).

Therefore we can conclude by saying:

1. When God appeared to certain people He had a physical form.

2. This form was not the essence of God but rather a physical representation of God for the benefit of those to whom He was speaking.

3. Nobody has seen God or can see God for, by nature, He is an invisible spirit.

WHAT DO THE VARIOUS NAMES OF GOD MEAN?

In the Hebrew Old Testament there are three basic names used for God from which many compounds are made. They are *Elohim, Adonai,* and *Yahweh.*

Elohim

The name commonly used for God in the Old Testament is *Elohim. Elohim* is used not only for the true God but also for false gods. The exact meaning of *Elohim* is not known though it seems to contain the idea of strength and power. The word is used in the first verse of the Bible:

In the beginning God (*Elohim*) created the heavens and the earth (Genesis 1:1).

The noun *Elohim* is plural but it is always used with a singular verb when its speaks of the true God. This indicates a unity and diversity within the nature of God which is revealed in Scripture as the doctrine of the Trinity.

Adonai

Another name used for God in the Old Testament is *Adonai* which means "Master" or "Lord." The term is not only applied to God, it is also used of men who master or lord over people. *Adonai* is often joined with *Elohim* indicating that God is the one who is Master and Lord and that we human beings are His subjects.

Yahweh (Jehovah)

Though *Elohim* and *Adonai* are applied to something other than the true and living God there is one name that is unique to the God of the Bible. This name is *Yahweh*—an alternative transliteration is *Jehovah*. Yahweh refers to "the self-existent, eternal God" the name God revealed to Moses:

And God said to Moses, I AM WHO I AM. And He said, 'Thus you shall say to the children of Israel, I AM has sent me to you' (Exodus 3:14).

He is *Yahweh* only to those who have a relationship with him. The name *Yahweh* is used throughout the Old Testament with compounds which describe something of His character. For example:

And Abraham called the name of the place, The-Lord-Will-Provide (*Yahweh-Yireh*) (Genesis 22:14).

Therefore the Lord says, The Lord of Hosts (*Yahweh-Sabaoth*), the Mighty One of Israel (Isaiah 1:24).

Now this is His name by which He will be called: THE LORD OUR RIGHTEOUSNESS (*Yahweh-Tsidkenu*) (Jeremiah 23:6).

In summing up we can say that:

1. The Hebrew Old Testament uses three basic names for God. They are *Elohim, Adonai,* and *Yahweh.*

2. These names are sometimes used with compounds which give insight into God's character.

3. The name *Elohim* means strength and might. It is also used of false gods.

4. The name *Adonai* means Lord and Master and can also refer to false gods.

5. The name *Yahweh* is the covenant name between God and His people. It is not used of false gods.

WHY IS GOD CALLED
THE FATHER?

The New Testament, time and time again, refers to God as the Father. Why? Does it mean that we are all children of God and that God is the Father of all mankind? In the New Testament we see to what extent that God is our Father.

First Person of the Trinity

As we have already noted, God, by nature, is a Trinity consisting of three distinct personalities, the Father, the Son, and the Holy Spirit. God the Father is the First Person of the Trinity, the one who sent and commissioned Jesus the Son to the earth. He is referred to as the Father of our Lord Jesus Christ:

Blessed be the God and Father of our Lord Jesus Christ, who has blessed us with every spiritual blessing in the heavenly places in Christ (Ephesians 1:3).

In the gospels we find the Father acknowledging Jesus as His Son:

And suddenly a voice came from heaven, saying, this is My beloved Son, in whom I am well pleased (Matthew 3:17).

The Son, likewise, acknowledges the Father:

All things have been delivered to Me by My Father, and no one knows the Son except the Father. Nor does anyone know the Father except the Son, and he to whom the Son wills to reveal Him (Matthew 11:27).

The terms Father and Son are used to describe the unique relationship between the first two Persons of the Trinity. The Bible makes it clear that both the Father and Son have existed together eternally. There was not a point in time when the Son came into being. Therefore we should not make an exact analogy between a human father and a human son when we speak of God the Father and God the Son. The terms are given to describe the unique oneness and unity that exists between these two Persons of the Godhead.

Father of All Who Believe

Another designation the Bible uses of the Father is that He is the Father of all those who put their faith in Him. The Scripture makes it clear that God is not the intimate Father of all mankind, He is only the Father to those who believe in Him. While it is true in a general sense that God is the Father, the Creator of every living thing, the intimate relationship a father has to his son is only experienced by those who believe.

The Bible explains the way one enters into this intimate father-son relationship with God is not through natural birth but through the new birth. This happens when an individual believes and puts his faith in Jesus Christ.

But to as many as received Him, to them He gave the right to become children of God, even to those who believe in His name (John 1:12).

For you are all sons of God through faith in Christ Jesus (Galatians 3:26).

Now, therefore, you are no longer strangers and foreigners, but fellow citizens with the saints and members of the household of God (Ephesians 2:19).

Father of All Creation

A third way in which the Bible designated God as the Father has to do with the created universe. He is the Father as the Creator, source, and sustainer of creation. The Apostle Paul said:

> For in Him we live and move and have our being, as also some of your own poets have said, 'For we are also his offspring,' Therefore, since we are the offspring of God, we ought not to think that the Divine Nature is like gold or silver or stone, something shaped by art and man's devising (Acts 17:28,29).

Therefore, in the Bible God is designated as the Father in the following ways:

1. God is called the Father as the first person in the Trinity. He is the eternal Father of Jesus Christ, God the Son. Theirs is a unique relationship.

2. God is the Father in an intimate relationship to all those who put their faith in Him.

3. God is the Father as the Creator and sustainer of all creation.

IS GOD THE FATHER A DISTINCT PERSON FROM GOD THE SON?

There are those who declare that God the Father and God the Son are the same person. They contend that the Son is merely a manifestation or development or role of the Father. The Bible, however, says that the Father and the Son are distinct from each other. They are not the same person. There are several ways in which the Bible illustrates this truth.

The Father is the Begetter: the Son is Begotten

The Son is spoken of as having been begotten by the Father. The word begotten means "unique," it does not contain the idea of coming into existence, of being born. Jesus is the only "unique" Son of God.

No one has seen God at any time. The only begotten Son, who is in the bosom of the Father, He has declared Him (John 1:18).

For God so loved the world that He gave His only begotten Son (John 3:16).

Here we have a distinction between the Father and Son. The Father is the begetter and the Son is the one begotten.

The Father Sent the Son

Another distinction we have between the Father and the Son is that the Father is the sender and the Son is the one sent.

Jesus said that it was God the Father who sent Him into the world:

> Do you say of Him who the Father sanctified and sent into the world, You are blaspheming, because I say I am the Son of God? (John 10:36).

The Apostle Paul also testified that the Father sent the Son into the world:

> But when the fulness of the time had come, God sent forth His Son, born of a woman, born under the law (Galatians 4:4).

The Father Testified to the Son

The Bible speaks of the Father testifying of the Son:

> If I bear witness of Myself, My witness is not true. There is another who bears witness of Me, and I know that the witness which He witnesses of Me is true . . . And the Father Himself, who sent Me, has testified of Me (John 5:31,32,37).

In this passage, Jesus is speaking to the religious leaders. He says that He is not the only one who is testifying concerning Himself. Jesus mentions the testimony of John the Baptist and the testimony of God the Father. Jesus contrasts His testimony from that of the Father showing that they are two distinct persons. The Father provides additional testimony to the character of Jesus.

The two divine persons—God the Father and God the Son—exist eternally and distinctly in an interpersonal relationship. For example, in the Garden of Gethsemane Jesus did not pray to Himself, but to the Father.

Therefore it is the teaching of Scripture that the Father is a distinct person from the Son in that:

1. The Son is begotten of the Father.

2. The Father sent the Son to earth.

3. The Father gave a testimony to the Son.

We also must mention that the Holy Spirit, the Third Person of the Trinity, is also distinct from the Father and the Son. Thus the Bible teaches that the three members of the Trinity, the Father, the Son, and the Holy Spirit, have eternally existed in an interpersonal relationship distinct from one another. (For more information on the Holy Spirit see *What Everyone Needs To Know About the Holy Spirit*, by Don Stewart, Orange, California, Dart Press, 1992).

WHAT ARE SOME INADEQUATE VIEWS OF GOD'S NATURE?

Throughout the history of the Christian church there have been other views brought forward to explain the nature of God that have fallen short of what the Bible says. Two of the most well-known are Unitarianism and Modalism.

UNITARIANISM

Unitarianism holds to the belief that God can not be properly spoken of as existing in three persons. God is rather a unity, one in essence and person.

Unitarianism dates back to the fourth century when Arius, a bishop from Alexandria, denied that Jesus was the eternal God. Arius taught that Jesus' nature was greater than man's but less than God's. He also denied that the Holy Spirit was God.

Modern Unitarianism dates from the sixteenth century to a man named Socinius. To Socinius, the death of Christ on the cross for the sins of mankind was unnecessary. Rather than believing that Jesus was a divine Savior, Socinius taught that God raised Jesus to divine power as an act of loving-kindness to His people.

Although they rejected the doctrine of the Trinity, the Unitarians of the seventeenth and eighteenth century viewed Jesus as one who had a special commission from God. They taught that Jesus revealed truth from God that man, through his reason, would not otherwise know. The nineteenth century saw a shift in the Unitarian position. Influenced by the German higher criticism of the Bible, a school of thought developed within Unitarianism that was antisupernatural. They came to doubt the four gospels as authoritative sources and rejected the uniqueness of Christianity. This rejection of Christianity's uniqueness was something that earlier Unitarian belief had also held. But with the antisupernaturalistic attitude, the goodness of man was stressed more than the existence and power of God.

Today Unitarianism does not ascribe to any set of beliefs. What binds Unitarians together is a basic belief in the goodness of man and that God is not limited to any one particular revelation, such as the Bible, but can be found in many different religions.

MODALISM

Modalism is another inadequate view of the nature of God. It teaches that God is one and that the three persons listed in the Bible, the Father, the Son, and the Holy Spirit are modes or manifestations of the one God. There are no separate persons within the nature of God from the modalistic point of view.

Originally the intent of Modalism was to preserve monotheism (that is the belief in the existence of the unity of the one God) while still holding to the divinity of Christ. But the Trinity of Modalism is a Trinity of manifestation. This means that the three personalities are expressions of the one person of God. The Trinity of the Bible is a Trinity of being which means the three persons are separate persons within the nature of the one God.

Modalism also undermines the Biblical teaching that God never changes for it portrays a God who changes His modes. The Bible pictures God as unchanging:

For I am the Lord, I do not change (Malachi 3:6).

Furthermore, Modalism takes away from the mediatorial work of Christ. The Bible teaches that Jesus is a mediator between God and man.

For there is one God and one Mediator between God and men, the Man Christ Jesus (1 Timothy 2:5).

The Modalistic view of God, that the Father and Son are the same person, would have God mediating between Himself. This is not biblical or logical.

We conclude that both Unitarianism and Modalism hold views of the Trinity that are inconsistent with biblical teaching.

CONCLUSION TO PART 2

From a careful study of what the Bible has to say we can conclude the following about the nature of God:

1. He is a personal being.

2. God is all-knowing. Nothing escapes His notice or knowledge.

3. He is everywhere present in the universe.

4. God is all-powerful. He is able to do anything that is consistent with His holy character.

5. God is a good God. He has demonstrated it in a variety of ways.

6. God cannot lie. When He promises something it will come to pass. We can rest assured that God's Word is good.

Now that we have seen what the Bible has to say about who God is, we will answer questions about what God has done. Why did God make man? Why does God allow evil? Did God create hell? Part 3 will concentrate on these and similar questions that deal with the works of God.

PART 3

GOD: HIS ACTS

For the Lord is the great King above all gods. In His hand are the deep places of the earth; the heights of the hills are His also. The sea is His, for He made it; and His hands formed the dry land.
—Psalm 95:3-5

DID GOD CREATE THE UNIVERSE?

What does the Bible say about how the universe came into existence? Did God create it? Did it evolve naturally? Or did God use evolutionary means to bring it about? The Bible is clear on this matter. The universe came into being by a series of creative acts by God.

God Is The Creator

Both the Old and New Testaments recognize God as the Creator.

In the beginning God created the heavens and the earth (Genesis 1:1).

All things were made by Him, and without Him nothing was made that was made (John 1:3).

For by Him all things were created that are in heaven and that are on earth, visible and invisible, whether thrones or dominions or principalities or powers. All things were created through Him and for Him (Colossians 1:16).

By faith we understand that the worlds were framed by the word of God, so that the things which are seen were not made of things which are visible (Hebrews 11:3).

The first chapter of Genesis makes about seventeen references to God as the Creator. The remainder of Scripture speaks of the creative works of God approximately fifty times. It is clear that the Bible teaches that God is the Creator of the universe.

Scripture also teaches that God created man. "So God created man in His own image; in the image of God He created him; male and female He created them" (Genesis 1:27).

The theory of evolution is at odds with the Biblical account of creation. Evolution teaches that everything developed by means of a slow, gradual change. All plants and animals developed from simple forms to more complex forms as a result of beneficial mutations. According to evolution man also developed in this way to reach his present complex form. The theory of evolution leaves no place for a creator.

God and Evolution?

There are some who attempt to unite the theory of evolution with a creator. This is called theistic evolution. This theory basically says that God used the evolutionary process to bring about the things as they are.

But theistic evolution contradicts what the Bible says. When God made man he was fully man at his creation.

> And the Lord God formed man of the dust of the ground, and breathed into his nostrils the breath of life; and man became a living being (Genesis 2:7).

This instantaneous creation of man shows that God did not use a long series of changes to bring man to his present state. Furthermore, God has demonstrated that He has sufficient power to create things instantly. Why take all the time that evolution requires to bring each species to their present form?

The Bible teaches that death is a result of sin. Before sin entered the world there was no death.

> Therefore, just as through one man sin entered the world, and death through sin, and thus death spread to all men . . (Romans 5:12).

If we are to accept the theistic evolutionary theory we would have to believe there were many deaths of animals and sub-human men before we got to Adam and the animals of the Garden of Eden. Yet the Bible says there was no death before Adam. The theory of theistic evolution, which wants the best of both worlds, does not do justice to the Bible (For a more detailed look at Theistic Evolution as well as other matters pertaining to the Bible and science see, Don Stewart, *What The Bible Says About Science,* Orange, California, Dart Press, 1992).

We therefore conclude:

1. The Bible teaches that man and the universe came about by special creative acts of God.

2. The theory of evolution, which teaches that everything is a result of slow, gradual change due to beneficial mutations in each of the species, is contrary to what the Bible says happened.

3. Theistic evolution would have God using the evolutionary method to create man. Yet this theory is contradicted by the testimony of Scripture.

COULD GOD HAVE CREATED THE WORLD AND THEN BACKED OFF?

There are those that hold a view of God's nature called deism. Deism believes that God created the world, set it in motion, but then backed off. The god of deism does not play an active role in his world but allows the universe to run by natural and self-sustaining laws that He established. Although the deists believe in a supernatural creation of the world, they do not believe in supernatural intervention in the world. Because there is no supernatural intervention by God, the deists believe that miracles do not occur. Hence they deny the miraculous accounts given in Scripture.

Deism is in contradiction to the God revealed in Scripture. If God can create the universe as the deists agree that He did, then He certainly is capable of performing other miracles of less magnitude. This is what the Bible says occurred. For example, God spoke to Moses in a bush that was burning with fire but the bush was not consumed. God guided the children of Israel supernaturally with a cloud by day and a pillar of fire by night. The Bible, from the first page until the last, is an account of God intervening miraculously in human history. To admit the miracle of creation and then to deny other miracles is an inconsistent position.

The most important miracle deism denies is the resurrection of Jesus Christ, upon which Christianity is based.

Master Clockmaker

The deist position would have God as a master "clockmaker." He made the clock, wound it, then left it alone. But the Bible portrays God as much more than a great "clockmaker." He is a loving Father who is personally interested in His children. God desires that humanity call out to Him when they have a need. The psalmist records God saying:

Call upon Me in the day of trouble; I will deliver you and you shall glorify Me (Psalm 50:15).

The deist position, that God created the universe but does not participate in the running of it, is contrary to what the Bible says.

WHY DID GOD CREATE MAN?

Oftentimes we hear people say that God created man because He needed someone to love. Does God need our love?

The answer is no. God does not need anything to exist. He is adequate in Himself. His existence is not dependent upon angels or man for He is complete in Himself. Jesus said of God the Father: "For as the Father has life in Himself" (John 5:26).

The Apostle Paul, while speaking to people on Mars Hill, affirmed God's self-existence.

> God, who made the world and everything in it, since He is Lord of heaven and earth, does not dwell in temples made with hands. Nor is He worshipped with men's hands, as though He needed anything, since He gives to all life, breath, and all things (Acts 17:24,25).

The adequacy of God is a theme that is found in both the Old and New Testaments. Those who mistakenly think that God created man because He needed love do not fully comprehend the situation. Before angels or man were created there was God. As we have already noted God is a Trinity comprised of Father, Son and Holy Spirit. Within the Trinity there was already love and communication. There was nothing lacking with God that made Him create man.

If that was the case then why was man created? Man was created to glorify God. Man was put on earth with a choice to trust God or to disobey Him. We have the opportunity to choose God and enjoy Him for all eternity. In that same speech on Mars Hill the Apostle Paul said:

And He has made us from one blood every nation of men to dwell on all the face of the earth, and has determined their preappointed times and the boundaries of their habitation, so that they should seek the Lord, in the hope that they may grope for Him and find Him, though He is not far from each one of us; for in Him we live and move and have our being (Acts 17:26-28).

This is why we were created. It was not for God's benefit, it was for ours. If we follow the instructions that God has given us, we can realize the purpose of our existence.

WHY DID GOD CREATE MAN IF HE KNEW THERE WOULD BE SO MUCH PAIN?

When God created the world and gave man a choice He knew that man would disobey Him. Since God knows everything He was aware that suffering and pain would follow. If this be the case then why did He create man in the first place? There are several options which God had.

God could have chosen not to create man at all. If He exercised this option then this would not be an issue.

God could have made man a robot without the ability to choose. If that be the case then there would not have been sin. There also would not have been choice. If everything were programmed then man would not have any significance. There would be no such thing as love or meaning to life. He would be no better than a machine.

Man Had a Choice

But God decided to make man with free will. Making choices is part of being a person. When He gave man choice the possibility of disobedience was real. When man disobeyed, pain and sorrow became a reality. But love, hope, and meaning to life also became real.

For man to have any significance he must have choice. Man exercised that choice and rebelled against God. This is why there is pain and suffering. God decided to create man with choice and to allow him to experience both the love and the hate, the pain and the suffering.

As to the why God created man with choice, He does not tell us. The Bible merely says that this is the manner in which God made man. God's ways are not the same as ours. The prophet Isaiah recorded God saying:

For My thoughts are not your thoughts, nor are your ways My ways, says the Lord. For as the heavens are higher than the earth, so are My ways higher than your ways, and My thoughts than your thoughts (Isaiah 55:8,9).

The Apostle Paul told the church at Rome:

Oh, the depth of the riches both of the wisdom and knowledge of God! How unsearchable are His judgments and His ways past finding out! (Romans 11:33).

DID GOD CREATE OTHER INHABITED WORLD'S APART FROM OUR OWN?

What does the Bible say about intelligent life existing on other planets besides earth?

On the issue of life on other worlds, the Bible does not give a specific answer. We are not told one way or the other whether there are other civilizations living elsewhere in the universe. Since the Bible is silent on this issue we must also remain silent.

Other Life

The Bible does speak about the existence of other intelligent life, but this is in the spirit world. These spirit beings are known as angels. The word translated *angel* comes from a Greek word meaning "messenger." The angels, who were created by God, serve as His messengers. Long ago one of the angels rebelled against God and took some of the other angels with him in his rebellion. This angel's name was Lucifer. Lucifer became Satan, or the Devil, when he rebelled against God. He and the other angels who followed him have been banished from God's presence. Yet these and the other angels do not constitute a civilization living elsewhere in the universe.

If there are other civilizations apart from our own, then the same moral laws would apply to them because God is unchanging in His moral character.

Whether God created another race like ours or a race totally different from our own we are not told. If we do discover another civilization, or are contacted by a different people, then it would not be contradictory with what the Bible says on the subject.

HOW INVOLVED IS GOD IN RUNNING THE UNIVERSE?

Though the Bible teaches that God created the universe some people question His involvement with it. There are those who claim that He is not involved with the orderly running of things. But the Bible speaks to the contrary. God supports and controls the universe He created:

Thus says the Lord, who gives the sun for a light by day, and the ordinances of the moon and the stars for a light by night, who disturbs the sea, and its waves roar (the Lord of hosts is His name) (Jeremiah 31:35).

If for one moment God stopped controlling and supporting the universe it would disintegrate. The Bible teaches that everything is dependent upon Him whether it be the change of seasons, the growth of plant and animal life, or the movement of the earth and stars.

He Holds Our Very Breath

The prophet Daniel told the pagan King Belshazzar that God holds our very breath in His hand.

You have praised the gods of silver and gold, bronze and iron, wood and stone, which do not see or hear or know; and the God who holds your breath in His hand and owns all your ways, you have not glorified (Daniel 5:23).

The New Testament tells us that it is Jesus Christ who holds all things in the universe together.

And He is before all things, and in Him all things consist (Colossians 1:17).

These Scriptures state that God is intimately involved in the functioning of the universe. His will is what holds everything together. Without His direct involvement the universe would cease to function.

DOES GOD PLAY AN ACTIVE ROLE IN THE AFFAIRS OF MANKIND?

God has made His presence felt among mankind since the beginning of time. Sometimes it has been obvious, sometimes not so obvious. He has revealed Himself in many different ways.

God revealed Himself to Moses in a burning bush that was not consumed.

> And the angel of the Lord appeared to him in a flame of fire from the midst of a bush. So he looked, and behold the bush burned with fire, but the bush was not consumed (Exodus 3:3).

God guided the children of Israel in a supernatural way.

> And the Lord went before them by day in a pillar of cloud to lead the way, and by night in a pillar of fire to give them light, so as to go by day and night (Exodus 13:21).

The people were aware that God was intimately involved in their lives. The prophet Amos said:

> If a trumpet is blown in a city, will not the people be afraid? If there is calamity in a city will not the Lord have done it? (Amos 3:6).

Jesus said that God is concerned about humanity:

> Are not two sparrows sold for a copper coin? And not one of them falls to the ground apart from your Father's will. But the very hairs on your head are all numbered. Do not fear therefore; you are of more value than many sparrows (Matthew 10:29-31).

God Sent His Son

The Bible is clear that God is intimately involved in the affairs of mankind. His greatest involvement was in sending His Son.

> God, who at various times and in different ways spoke in time past to the fathers by the prophets, has in these last days spoken to us by His Son, whom He has appointed heir to all things, through whom also He made the worlds; who being the brightness of His glory and the express image of His person, and upholding all things by the word of His power, when He had by Himself purged our sins, sat down at the right hand of the Majesty on high (Hebrews 1:1-3).

> For God so loved the world that He gave His only begotten Son, that whoever believes in Him should not perish but have everlasting life (John 3:16).

DID GOD CREATE MAN AS A
REBELLIOUS CREATURE?

Mankind is in a state of rebellion against the God who created Him. Though man may recognize that God exists, he fails to live up to the standards that God has set down. Is this the way God created man? Was he made to be rebellious? The Bible says man became rebellious against God due to his choice rather than having been created that way by God.

It was God's desire that man depend upon and obey Him. When Adam was created he was given a choice to obey or disobey God:

> And the Lord God commanded the man, saying, 'Of every tree of the garden you may freely eat; but of the tree of the knowledge of good and evil you shall not eat, for in the day you eat of it you shall surely die' (Genesis 2:16,17).

Man chose to act independently of God. When Adam and his wife, Eve, ate of the fruit of the tree God had commanded them not to eat, they brought sin into the universe. The Apostle Paul commented upon their action,

> Therefore, just as through one man sin entered into the world, and death through sin, and thus death spread to all men, because all sinned—(Romans 5:12).

Thus it was man who brought the rebellion upon himself by disobeying the commandment of God. His rebellion also brought the consequence of sin. This was not what God wanted or desired. He warned man what would happen should he disobey, but man rebelled nevertheless. Our rebellious nature cannot be blamed upon God, but upon Adam and Eve for rebelling against God in the beginning.

WHAT DOES IT MEAN: MAN WAS MADE IN THE IMAGE OF GOD?

The Bible speaks of man being created in the image of God:

> So God created man in His own image; in the the image of God He created him; male and female He created them (Genesis 1:27).

> In the day that God created man. He made him in the likeness of God. He created them male and female, and blessed them and called them Mankind in the day they were created (Genesis 5:1,2).

What does it mean that man was created in God's image? To say that man was made in the image of God means that God and man have many things in common. When God created man He gave him such things as personality, choice, emotions, morality, and creativity.

Personality

Both man and God have personality. That is to say they can both think and communicate as rational beings. They each have personal identity that is separate from other rational beings and from nonliving things. Man and God also have the ability to communicate to other rational beings. The Bible says:

And have put on the new man who is renewed in knowledge according to the image of Him who created him (Colossians 3:10).

Choice

A second common trait between man and God is choice. Both God and man are beings that have the ability to choose, though God does not have the ability to choose evil. Neither God nor man are programmed or forced to make any choices. This freedom was given to man by God and man is responsible for the choices he makes.

Man and God both have emotions. For example, each can give love and receive love. God, as well as man, can be angry. Both man and God have the capacity to feel and express emotions.

Man and God both have a moral sense of right and wrong. Each knows and understands the difference between good and evil. The Bible says:

And that you put on the new man which was created according to God, in righteousness and true holiness (Ephesians 4:24).

Another attribute that God and man have in common is creativity. The Bible says God created the universe and everything within it. Man also is a creative being having been given this ability by God.

The image of God that man was created in is a moral and intellectual image. Man was given many of the traits that God possesses.

WHAT IS GOD'S RELATIONSHIP TO THE NATION ISRAEL?

Of all the nations that have existed upon the earth, God has chosen to work specifically through one, the nation Israel.

Through He loves all of mankind, God set up a special relationship between Himself and Israel.

Chosen People

The Jews are God's chosen people. They were specially chosen by God to be a witness of Him to the unbelieving world. It was to Israel that the Word of God came. The Apostle Paul wrote:

> What advantage then has the Jew, or what is the profit of circumcision? Much in every way! Chiefly because to them were committed the oracles of God (Romans 3:1,2).

> I tell the truth in Christ, I am not lying, my conscience also bearing me witness in the Holy Spirit, that I have great sorrow and continual grief in my heart. For I could wish that I myself were accursed from Christ for my brethren, to whom pertain the adoption, the glory, the covenants, the giving of the law, the service of God, and the promises; of whom are the fathers and from whom, according to the flesh, Christ came who is over all, the eternally blessed God. Amen (Romans 9:1-5).

Israel had the great privilege of receiving God's revelation to mankind. It was to the Israelites that the prophets of God appeared. As God's chosen people they were to be witnesses to the true and living God in the land which God gave them.

Based Upon God's Choice

Yet the Bible makes it clear that God chose Israel to be His instrument because of His own intentions; it was not because Israel was better than any other nation.

Therefore understand that the Lord your God is not giving you this good land to possess because of your righteousness, for you are a stiff-necked people (Deuteronomy 9:6).

Israel was given many special blessings from God. Along with them came a great responsibility to keep those things God had entrusted to them. When they failed to keep their godly testimony to the world they were judged by God. Jesus made it clear that great blessings meant great responsibility.

For everyone to whom much is given, from him much will be required; and to whom much has been committed, of him they will ask the more (Luke 12:48).

The Present Situation

God is no longer using the nation Israel as His means of testifying to the unbelieving world. Rather than having a national witness in the land of Palestine, where all nations can see God working through a people, He is now sending His Word out through His believers. Jesus said that those who believe in Him are now to go out and preach the good news.

Go therefore and make disciples of all the nations, baptizing them in the name of the Father and of the Son and of the Holy Spirit (Matthew 28:19).

Thus we can conclude that what the Bible says about God's relationship with the Jews includes:

1. God chose Israel to be His special representative to the world. In this sense they are the "chosen people."

2. God's relationship with Israel was based upon God's choice, not Israel's faithfulness.

3. The Israelites were to be a witness to the truth of God. When they failed in their witness God judged them.

Today, rather than working through one particular nation, God is sending His Word out by means of the body of Christ, Christians.

HAS GOD BEEN FAITHFUL TO ISRAEL?

We have seen that God made promises to the nation Israel regarding their right to the promised land and their survival. What is the verdict of history? Has God been faithful to the promises He made?

When history is examined it is evident that God has remained faithful to His promises.

Through the leader Joshua, God brought Israel into the land which he had promised. But the people did not remain obedient to Him.

In 931 B.C. the nation split into two kingdoms. The northern part consisted of ten tribes and was known as Israel. The southern kingdom consisted of two tribes and became known as Judah.

Removal

Because of the people's continual sin, the northern kingdom of Israel was taken into captivity in 721 B.C. by the Assyrians.

The people of Judah also sinned against God and they were taken captive by the Babylonians in 606 B.C. The city of Jerusalem and the temple were destroyed in 586 B.C.

God had promised that sin would cause His people's removal from the land. But God also promised that He would bring them back. After a seventy-year captivity the Jews returned to the promised land in 536 B.C.

Removed Again

They were, however, removed from their land a second time. In A.D. 70, Titus, the Roman, surrounded the city of Jerusalem and destroyed the rebuilt city and temple. Again the people were scattered.

Yet against incredible odds God again demonstrated His faithfulness to the nation Israel. After wandering the earth for almost two thousand years they again became a sovereign state in that land. On May 14, 1948, the modern state of Israel was reborn.

No other nation has ever been removed once from its homeland and returned. It has happened twice to the nation Israel. The first time was for seventy years, the second time for almost two thousand years. God promised that He would remain faithful to Israel and the verdict of history is clear. Israel's survival is a testimony to the faithfulness of God (For further documentation see Don Stewart, *Ten Reasons To Trust The Bible*, Orange, California, Dart Press, 1990).

DOES GOD EVER
GET ANGRY?

There are people who assume that since God is a God of love He would never get angry at anything or anybody. But when one reads the Bible he discovers that God does get angry, He gets angry at sin. God's anger, however, is always under control and is always righteous.

God is portrayed in a variety of images that express anger at sin.

Behold, the name of the Lord comes from afar, burning with anger, and His burden is heavy; His lips are full of indignation, and His tongue like a devouring fire; His breath is like an overflowing stream, which reaches up to the neck, to sift the nations with the sieve of futility (Isaiah 30:27,28).

Anger Toward Individuals

Sometimes God's anger is vented toward individuals. There are other times when He is angry at the nation Israel, and on other occasions His wrath is against those nations who try to destroy Israel. The psalmist records God's anger at the individual:

Your fierce wrath has gone over me; Your terrors have cut me off (Psalm 88;16).

Anger Toward Israel

God expressed anger at the nation Israel for disobeying Him.

> And the Lord said to Moses, 'I have seen this people, and indeed it is a stiffnecked people! Now therefore, let Me alone, that My wrath may burn hot against them' (Exodus 32:9,10).

Anger Toward the Nations

The prophet Ezekiel records God's anger at Philistia, one of the nations seeking to destroy Israel:

> I will execute great vengeance on them with furious rebukes; then they shall know that I am the Lord, when I lay My vengeance upon them (Ezekiel 25:17).

Since God is a God of love why would He be so offended at sin? It must be remembered that God is also righteous and holy. Sin is offensive to God because His nature is one of perfection.

Mercy

We must stress, however, that God is a God of mercy and forgiveness. When individuals or nations repent of their sin God is willing and able to forgive them of that sin. His anger turns to forgiveness when people come to Him with humble hearts. God has said:

> The instant that I speak concerning a nation and concerning a kingdom, to pluck up, to pull down, and to destroy it, if that nation against whom I have spoken turns from its evil, I will relent of the disaster that I thought to bring upon it. And the instant I speak concerning a nation and concerning a kingdom, to build and to plant it, if it does evil in My sight so that it does not obey My voice, then I will relent concerning the good with which I said I would benefit from it (Jeremiah 18:7-10).

We can conclude by saying:

1. God is a being perfect in His character.

2. Sin offends His perfect character.

3. When nations or individuals reject His love and goodness, God becomes angry at them.

4. When there is genuine repentance God forgives the sinning party.

HOW HAS GOD PUNISHED SIN?

Sin has not only made God angry, it is something that God has judged. Before sin entered the universe God established unchangeable laws. One of these laws was that sin had to be punished. When sin entered the world God proceeded to punish it. The Bible gives us examples of God punishing sin.

Sometimes He judged sin by sending a natural disaster.

Now when the people complained, it displeased the Lord; for the Lord heard it, and His anger was aroused. So the fire of the Lord burned among them, and consumed some in the outskirts of the camp (Numbers 11:1).

On another occasion God judged sin by sending disease upon those who offended Him.

So the anger of the Lord was aroused against them, and He departed. And when the cloud departed from above the tabernacle, suddenly Miriam became leprous, as white as snow (Numbers 12:9,10).

A great example of God's judging of sin is the sending of the nation Israel into the captivity at Babylon. Because of their continued sin God sent them into a seventy-year captivity.

A God of Mercy

But the judgment of sin is something that God does not enjoy doing. God would rather grant mercy. In the three cases mentioned God showed His great mercy on the people that He had judged.

After fire was sent into the camp of the children of Israel, Moses prayed to the Lord and the fire was quenched.

Miriam was also cured of leprosy because of prayer on her behalf.

The children of Israel were allowed to return to their homeland after the seventy years of Babylonian captivity.

We see that God has judged sin in the past but that He would rather grant mercy to those who ask His forgiveness.

WHY DID GOD ORDER THE DESTRUCTION OF THE CANAANITES?

One of the difficult problems posed by events recorded in the Book of Joshua in the Old Testament concerns the destruction of the Canaanites. When the children of Israel entered the Promised Land they destroyed the Canaanites as ordered by the Lord. The Bible tells what happened when the Israelites conquered Jericho:

> And they utterly destroyed all that was in the city, both man and woman, young and old, ox and sheep and donkey, with the edge of the sword (Joshua 6:21).

Why did God order everyone destroyed including women, children, and animals? Does this not show a cruel and warlike attitude?

While the loss of innocent life is something that is to be deplored, the situation must be understood with the following background in mind. The nation Israel was chosen to be a witness to the world of the true and living God. The Israelites were to live in the Promised Land surrounded by the heathen nations, yet they were not to be influenced by the other nations' religions. God instructed His people that they were not to take to themselves any of the elements of the false pagan religions.

The Promised Land in which the Israelites were to settle was populated by the Canaanites who had corrupted and perverted God's truth. They had corrupted themselves to the place where they were beyond saving. Had any been permitted to live, they would have infected Israel with their moral depravity.

Before Israel could establish itself in the region as a witness to the one true God, all remnants of the pagan culture had to be destroyed. The failure to totally eliminate all of the pagans in the Promised Land eventually led to the nation's downfall in the times of the Judges.

> Then the angel of the Lord came to Gilgal to Bochim, and said: I led you up from Egypt and brought you to the land of which I swore to your fathers; and I said, I will never break My covenant with you. And you shall make no covenant with the inhabitants of this land; you shall tear down their altars. But you have not obeyed My voice. Why have you done this? Therefore I also said, I will not drive them out before you; but they shall be thorns in your side, and their gods shall be a snare to you (Judges 2:1-3).

God ordered the destruction of the Canaanites because of the corrupting influence they would have if their false religious system were allowed to survive. Unfortunately, Israel disobeyed God and did not utterly destroy these pagan peoples. This disobedience eventually led to their own captivity.

Innocent Victims?

The people that lived in Canaan were not ignorant of the God of Israel. Many times the impression is given that God ordered the Israelites to swoop in and destroy innocent people. But these people were neither innocent nor ignorant. They had heard about the God of Israel but had rejected Him.

When two spies were sent to spy out the Land of Promise they were told by Rahab the harlot,

> I know that the Lord has given you the land, that the terror of you has fallen on us and that all the inhabitants of the land are fainthearted because of you. For we have heard how the Lord dried up the water of the Red Sea for you when you came out of Egypt, and what you did to the two kings of the Amorites who were on the other side of the Jordan, Sihon, and Og, whom you utterly destroyed. And as soon as we heard these things, our hearts melted; neither did there remain any more courage in anyone

because of you, for the Lord your God, He is God in heaven above and on earth beneath (Joshua 2:11).

They had heard of the true God but had rejected Him. Consequently, their entire society acted in a sinful way. The Apostle Paul spoke of these people:

Although they knew God, they did not glorify Him as God, nor were thankful, but became futile in their thoughts, and their foolish hearts were darkened. Professing to be wise, they became fools, and changed the glory of the incorruptible God into an image made like corruptible man—and birds and four-footed beasts and creeping things. Therefore God also gave them up to uncleanness, in the lusts of their hearts, to dishonor their bodies among themselves, who exchanged the truth of God for the lie, and worshipped the creature rather than the Creator (Romans 1:21-25).

The inhabitants of Canaan were neither ignorant nor innocent victims of an angry God. They had been committing terrible sin knowing full well of the true and living God. Because they rejected Him and His forgiveness they were judged for their sin.

HAS GOD PERFORMED
MIRACLES?

The Bible indicates that God has broken into human history and performed miraculous deeds. The Bible, from beginning to end, testifies to the miraculous acts of God.

What is a miracle? The word *miracle* is used in two different ways. In the first instance it is used to describe an unusual or natural event that occurs at a precise time. This is usually in answer to prayer. The miracle is in the timing of the event.

The New Testament gives the example of a miraculous catch of fish.

But when the morning had now come, Jesus stood on the shore; yet the disciples did not know it was Jesus. Then Jesus said to them, 'Children, have you any food?' They answered Him, 'No.' and He said to them, 'Cast the net on the right side of the boat, and you will find some.' So they cast, and now they were not able to draw it in because of the multitude of fish (John 21:4-6).

There is nothing miraculous about casting a net into the water and having it filled with fish. This event, however, was a miracle because they had been fishing all night and had not caught a thing. But when Jesus told where to put their net it immediately became full.

Another example of a miracle of this order is the feeding of Elijah by the ravens. God told Elijah:

> Get away from here and turn eastward, and hide by
> the Brook Cherith, which flows into Jordan. And it will be
> that you shall drink from the brook, and I have
> commanded the ravens to feed you there. So he went and
> did according to the word of the Lord, for he went and
> stayed by the Brook Cherith, which flows into the
> Jordan. The ravens brought him bread and meat in the
> morning, and bread and meat in the evening; and he
> drank from the brook (1 Kings 17:3-6).

Though God did not suspend the laws of nature when
He fed Elijah by the ravens it certainly was a series of
miraculously timed events.

Events like these are not contrary to the laws of
science; nonetheless, they are miracles of timing and place.

Beyond Natural Law

The Bible speaks of a second type of miracle performed
by God. This kind of miracle cannot be explained in terms
of normal cause and effect.

Jesus walking on water is an example of this kind of
totally supernatural miracle.

> Now in the fourth watch of the night Jesus went to
> them, walking on the sea (Matthew 14:25).

This miracle cannot be explained by the normal laws of
science because it is physically impossible for people to
walk on water.

Feeding of Five Thousand

Another example of this type of miracle is Jesus
feeding the five thousand. When a multitude of people who
had followed Jesus became hungry, Jesus took the food
that was available—five loaves and two fish—and
miraculously turned it into enough food to feed the great
crowd. The Bible says:

> So when they all ate and were filled, and they took up
> twelve baskets full of fragments that remained. Now
> those who had eaten were about five thousand men,
> besides women and children (Matthew 14:20,21).

Not only did everyone eat, all were filled and the
disciples gathered baskets full of leftovers. This miracle
cannot be explained by the normal laws of cause and effect.

Both the Old and New Testaments testify to God performing many miracles. These miracles were either unusual events that occurred at God's precise timing, or events beyond the normal laws of nature and science. In either case, the miracles are convincing evidence of God's great power and His control over the laws He established when He created the universe.

Why Did God Perform Miracles?

We have seen that there is evidence that the God of the Bible has broken into history by performing miraculous deeds. What was the purpose of His miracles?

The word translated *miracle* can also mean "sign." The miracles that were performed by God were done as signs to testify to His existence and power.

Purpose

The Apostle John testified why he recorded Jesus' miracles.

And truly Jesus did many other signs in the presence of His disciples, which are not written in this book; but these are written that you may believe that Jesus is the Christ, the Son of God, and that believing you may have life in His name (John 20:30,31).

God speaks of His miraculous deeds as signs to the people.

I will show wonders in heaven above and signs in the earth beneath: blood and fire and vapor of smoke (Acts 2;19).

The signs that Jesus performed convinced many that He was the Messiah.

Now when He was in Jerusalem at the Passover, during the feast, many believed in His name when they saw the signs which He did (John 2:23).

Some Doubted

Yet even with the miraculous signs there were some who doubted. After Jesus' resurrection there were still some who did not believe.

And when they saw Him, they worshipped Him, but some doubted (Matthew 28:17).

The miracles of the Bible were performed as signs to testify of God's existence and power. And although the signs convinced many, there were still some who doubted.

WHY BELIEVE THE BIBLICAL MIRACLES? DON'T OTHER RELIGIONS CLAIM THE SAME THING?

Why believe the biblical miracles? What makes them so special? There are many religions who claim miracles as having happened to verify the truth of their faith. Do not the miracles performed in other religions testify to the existence of other gods?

When the facts are considered it will be discovered that the biblical miracles are on a different level than those of other religions and consequently are the only ones that are to be believed.

Eyewitness Testimony

The miracles performed in the Bible are substantiated with eyewitness testimony. Those who saw the miraculous events are the same people who recorded them. John the evangelist wrote:

> That which was from the beginning, which we have heard, which we have seen with our eyes, which we have looked upon, and our hands have handled, concerning the Word of life (1 John 1:1).

Simon Peter echoed the same thought:

For we did not follow cunningly devised fables when we
made known to you the power and coming of our Lord
Jesus Christ, but were eyewitnesses of His majesty (2
Peter 1:16).

On the day of Pentecost Peter said to the large
audience that had gathered:

Men of Israel, hear these words: Jesus of Nazareth, a
Man attested by God to you by miracles, wonders, and
signs which God did through Him in your midst, as you
yourselves also know (Acts 2:22).

Simon Peter appealed to the knowledge of his hearers.
They were aware that Jesus had performed miraculous
works.

Not Done in a Corner

The miracles of the Bible were done publicly. The
Apostle Paul said:

I am not mad, most noble Festus, but speak the words
of truth and reason. For the king, before whom I also
speak freely, knows these things; for I am convinced that
none of these things escapes his attention, since this
thing was not done in a corner (Acts 26:25,26).

Done For a Specific Purpose

Whenever God performed a miracle it was always done
for a specific purpose. The miracles were performed as
signs to testify of God's existence and power or to meet a
specific need. They were never performed as a sideshow or
to merely attract attention.

The parting of the Red Sea is an example of a biblical
miracle performed for a particular purpose. When the
children of Israel were caught by Pharoah's army at the
Red Sea God miraculously delivered them by dividing the
waters of the sea. This act testified to the power of God and
met a specific need that the people had—namely to be
saved from the oncoming Egyptian army.

When Jesus was being tempted by the devil He refused
to use His miraculous powers to show off. The devil wanted
Jesus to throw Himself down from the pinnacle of the
temple and let the angels miraculously save Him, but Jesus
would not stoop to this type of supernatural sideshow. He

performed miracles to meet real human needs, not to draw a crowd.

Other Miracle Stories Fail

The miracles attributed to other religions fail on both these levels. They are not backed up by eyewitness testimony, and they are all too often performed as a sideshow with no direct purpose in mind. The so-called miracles of other religions do not touch humanity at its basic needs as do the miracles recorded in the Bible. Consequently they are to be rejected.

We conclude about biblical miracles:

1. They were performed in the sight of eyewitnesses to verify their accuracy.

2. The miracles were always done for a specific purpose, never to show off.

3. The miracles attributed to other religions do not have the same type of verification.

WHAT ABOUT MODERN DAY MIRACLES?

The Bible records many miracles performed by the power of God. What about today? Does God still perform miracles?

Same God

God is still the same God as He was from the beginning and He does possess the power to perform miracles. However, when a person examines the program of God as revealed in the Bible, he finds that miracles were never the norm. They were the exception to the rule. Miracles were performed to demonstrate God's existence and power, or to meet a specific need.

When Jesus Christ came to earth, God made His final statement to mankind before Jesus comes again. Through Jesus, and those who wrote about Him, God has given us an objective account of what He requires of us in order that we may know Him.

Faith in Christ

Today, God asks people to place their faith in Jesus Christ based upon what He has done for them on the cross at Calvary. We should not expect any more miraculous signs, such as God suspending the laws of nature, to verify what Christ has done.

Future Miracles

We know that when Christ returns there will be miracles surrounding that event. Miracles are still a part of God's future program.

We do not want to limit God and say what He can or cannot do. Modern day miracles are certainly possible but they should not be expected as normative. God does not have to prove Himself over and over again by performing miracles. He has demonstrated His existence and power once and for all through the person of Jesus Christ.

WILL GOD ALLOW THE WORLD TO BE DESTROYED?

The world in which we live is in a very precarious situation. The danger of a nuclear war that could destroy our planet is a very real threat. Does the Bible have anything to say about this matter? Will God allow the world to be destroyed?

World will Survive

Although it may seem that man will inevitably blow the world to pieces, the Bible says otherwise. God is not going to allow this to happen, because Jesus will return to earth a second time before man can destroy himself.

We know this because according to biblical prophecy when Christ comes back to earth to set up His kingdom, there will be people living on the earth:

> Then the sign of the Son of Man will appear in heaven, and then all the tribes of the earth will mourn, and they will see the Son of Man coming on the clouds of heaven with power and great glory. And He will send His angels with a great sound of a trumpet, and they will gather together His elect from the four winds, from one end of heaven to another (Matthew 24:30,31).

> Behold, He is coming with clouds and every eye will see Him, and they also who pierced Him. And all the tribes of the earth will mourn because of Him (Revelation 1:7).

All of these verses assume people are living upon the earth when Christ returns. The Bible speaks of the people on earth mourning and that every eye shall see Him. This necessitates people being on earth at that time. Scripture does not support the possibility of mankind destroying himself before God intervenes.

Jesus said His second coming would prevent people from destroying themselves:

> For then there will be great tribulation, such as has not been since the beginning of the world until this time, no, nor ever shall be. And unless those days were shortened, no flesh would be saved; but for the elect's sake those days will be shortened (Matthew 24:21,22).

Though God promises man will not destroy himself, that fact does not relieve us of our responsibility. We should be diligent in our actions to procure and sustain peaceful relations with individuals and the nations of the world.

Thus we can conclude:

1 The Bible teaches that God will not let man destroy the world.

2 Christ said He will return to prevent mankind's destruction.

WILL GOD SEND
PEOPLE TO HELL?

The Bible speaks about a place of final judgment for those who do not believe in the salvation provided by Jesus Christ. This place is known as hell. It is not a geographical place, but a state of existence. Jesus spoke of it as a place of eternal punishment.

And these will go away into everlasting punishment (Matthew 25:46).

Final Judgment

In the Book of Revelation the Apostle John wrote concerning a final judgment of the wicked:

And I saw the dead, small and great, standing before God, and the books were opened. And another book was opened, which is the Book of Life. And the dead were judged according to their works, by the things which were written in the books. . . And anyone not found written in the Book of Life was cast into the lake of fire (Revelation 20:12,15).

The reality of a final judgment is clearly taught in Scripture. But the Bible also indicates that the people who go to hell do so because they have rejected God's provision for salvation. The Bible says that God does not want anyone to go to hell:

The Lord is not slack concerning His promise, as some count slackness, but is longsuffering toward us, not willing that any should perish but that all should come to repentance (2 Peter 3:9).

Thus we conclude by saying:

1. The Bible teaches the reality of a final place of judgment for the wicked.

2. Those who spend eternity in hell do so because they rejected God's love and His provision for salvation.

3. It is God's desire for everyone to come to Him by faith and receive the salvation that He offers.

63

WHY DID GOD
CREATE HELL?

If it is God's sincere desire that everyone come to know Him why did He create hell in the first place? Why make a place of judgment for humanity?

The Bible teaches that God did not create hell as a judgment for humanity. God created hell for the punishment of the devil and his angels and not as a place for human beings to suffer. Jesus said:

> Then He will also say to those on the left hand, 'Depart from Me, you cursed, into the everlasting fire prepared for the devil and his angels' (Matthew 25:41).

Hell was created as a place of judgment for Satan and those who followed him in their rebellion against God. The Bible says that the devil and his angels will eventually be consigned to hell:

> And the devil who deceived them, was cast into the lake of fire and brimstone where the beast and false prophet are. And they will be tormented day and night forever and ever (Revelation 20:10).

Human beings, who are created in God's image, are not meant to spend eternity away from the presence of God. The place God created for them is heaven. Jesus spoke of this place that God has prepared for those who trust Him:

In My Father's house are many mansions: if it were not so, I would have told you. I go to prepare a place for you. And if I go and prepare a place for you, I will come again and receive you to Myself; that where I am, there you may be also (John 14:2,3).

Hell was not created for humanity, but it is the destination for those who reject God's salvation in Jesus Christ.

HOW CAN THE EXISTENCE OF HELL BE RECONCILED WITH A LOVING GOD?

Some people wonder how hell can be reconciled with a God of love. Why, they ask, would a God of love allow people to go to hell?

God of Justice

The answer to this question is that God is a God of holiness and justice as well as a God of love. These moral attributes are complementary, not contradictory. When the laws of God are disobeyed there must be a judgment. God's laws demand that sin must be paid for. God can still love someone but He cannot allow sin to go unpunished. This is the reason that Jesus Christ came to earth, to die for the sins of the world.

Just as the Son of Man did not come to be served, but to serve, and to give His life a ransom for many (Matthew 20:28).

The emphasis should not be placed upon hell but by the fact that God came to earth in the person of Jesus Christ to show His love for mankind:

For when we were without strength, in due time Christ died for the ungodly. For scarcely for a righteous man will one die; yet perhaps for a good man someone would even dare to die. But God demonstrates His own love toward us, in that while we were still sinners, Christ died for us (Romans 5:6-8).

God has showed His love by sending His Son to die for our sins—to take our punishment—so that we could go to heaven. The judgment of hell is for those who refuse to accept God's love and forgiveness.

DID GOD
CREATE EVIL?

If God created all things does this include evil? If so, why did He do it? Would that not make Him a bad God?

It is true that if God created evil it would make Him a bad God. But this is not the case. Evil came as a result of sin, and sin is something that God did not want in the universe.

The origin of evil lies not with God but with man. When God created human beings He gave them a choice to obey or disobey. When Adam and Eve chose to disobey God they brought evil into the universe. Evil is an action or relationship, not a created substance.

God did not create evil and neither is He to blame for the evil in the universe. God could have made people in such a way that they would be robots who would react when God made them do so. But that would not give humanity any significance. God decided to make people in such a way that they could choose whether or not to obey Him.

Choice of Man

Furthermore, much of the evil in the universe is due to the direct choice of individuals. Murder, stealing, lying, and such cannot be blamed upon God. People choose to do these things and must be held accountable.

Though natural disasters such as earthquakes and famines are not caused by man, he is indirectly

responsible for their occurrence. They occur as a result of man's sin. When sin entered the universe everything was affected. The perfect working order is now tainted by sin.
Therefore we can conclude by saying:

1. God did not create evil. Evil came as a result of man's choice.

2. God cannot be blamed for the evil that continues. Man is directly or indirectly responsible for evil.

WHY DOES GOD ALLOW EVIL TO EXIST?

If God is a good God then why is there evil in the universe? Is it because God is not good, or is it because God is not powerful enough to deal with evil? Asking this question infers God is either unable or unwilling to deal with evil. But neither is the case.

God is certainly able to do something about evil. The Bible teaches that God is all-powerful.

> Behold, I am the Lord, the God of all flesh. Is there anything too hard for Me? (Jeremiah 32:27).

The fact that God is powerful enough to deal with evil is not the issue. He has demonstrated time and time again that He has the capability to end evil.

God is also a God of love who cares for His people. The Scripture teaches that God always has the best interest of humanity in mind in every decision that He makes.

He Will Do Something

The answer is that God will do something about evil, but it will be in His perfect time. God has a plan by which He is running this earth. One of the things in God's plan is to end evil and the fruits of evil.

> And God shall wipe away every tear from their eyes; there shall be no more death, nor sorrow, nor crying; and

there shall be no more pain, for the former things have passed away (Revelation 21:4).

There will be an end to evil when God has finished dealing with mankind.

DID GOD CREATE
THE DEVIL?

One of the accusations that is often hurled at God is that He created the devil who in turned caused immeasurable suffering for mankind. Why would God create such a creature? But does the Bible say that He created the devil? The answer is no. The biblical account is as follows:

Before the creation of man and the earth everything in the universe was in harmony with God. God had created angels or spirit beings who had duties to perform. Each of them was given a rank. One of the highest ranked of all the angels was one named Lucifer.

One day Lucifer decided to break this harmonious relationship with God. He decided that he wanted to be like God. The Bible has this to say of what transpired:

How are you fallen from heaven, O Lucifer, son of the morning! How are you cut down to the ground, you who weakened the nations! For you have said in your heart: 'I will ascend into heaven, I will exalt my throne above the stars of God; I will also sit on the mount of the congregation on the farthest sides of the north; I will ascend above the heights of the clouds, I will be like the Most High' (Isaiah 14:12).

It is recorded in this passage that Lucifer willed something contrary to God five different times. This was the first time that any creature in the universe rebelled against God. Pride was the sin that caused Lucifer to lose his exalted position and be cast out of heaven. He became Satan or the adversary. He was not created as the Devil but he chose that route for himself.

Thus the Scriptures say that:

1 God's universe was created in perfect harmony.

2 The angels, who were part of God's creation, were subject to God's will.

3 A high-ranking angel named Lucifer decided he wanted to be like God.

4 This act of rebellion brought sin into the universe.

5 Lucifer then became the Devil, Satan, the adversary of God.

6 God, therefore, did not create the devil, nor did he wish him to rebel. The devil made his own choice.

WHY DIDN'T GOD DESTROY THE DEVIL WHEN HE FIRST REBELLED?

Even though God did not create the devil, He still had the capacity to destroy him when he first rebelled. Why did God allow the devil to survive and bring so much misery upon mankind?

The Bible does not give a direct answer to this question. We do not know the mind of God on this matter. But there are some principles that the Bible gives that may help us understand why God did not immediately destroy the devil.

Within the eternal plan of God the chaos caused by the devil can be used to glorify God. The Scripture has said,

> Surely the wrath of man shall praise You (Psalm 76:10).

How this is accomplished we do not know. But the Scripture tells us that God's ways are above ours.

> For My thoughts are not your thoughts, nor are your ways My ways, says the Lord. For as the heavens are higher than the earth, so are My ways higher than your ways, and My thoughts than your thoughts (Isaiah 55:8,9).

Finally we must point out that the devil will eventually be judged. The Bible records his inglorious end.

And the devil, who deceived them, was cast into the lake of fire and brimstone where the beast and the false prophet are. And they will be tormented day and night forever and ever (Revelation 20:10).

God's Word does not tell why God did not immediately destroy Satan. His ways are higher than ours. But He does tell us that the devil will eventually be destroyed. The time of his destruction is in the perfect plan of God.

DO THE TWO TESTAMENTS PORTRAY DIFFERENT CONCEPTS OF GOD?

There are those who read the Bible and seem to find different concepts of God in the two testaments. They say the Old Testament portrays a God of wrath and judgment, while the New Testament pictures a God of love who will not judge mankind. These two portrayals of God are, to some people, incompatible.

But this is not the case. The character of God as revealed in the Bible is consistent throughout. The Old Testament does not portray a primitive God of anger who delights in judging His people. Furthermore, the New Testament does not portray a God of love who refuses to judge sin.

In the Old Testament God made it clear that He loved His people.

> The Lord has appeared of old to me, saying: 'Yes, I have loved you with an everlasting love' (Jeremiah 31:3).

Jesus said that the Old Testament law and prophets could be summed up as follows:

> 'You shall love the Lord your God with all your heart, with all your soul, and with all your mind.' This is the first and greatest commandment. And the second is like it: 'You shall love your neighbor as yourself.' On these two

commandments hang all the Law and Prophets (Matthew 22:37-39).

Though the Old Testament contains statements of God judging sin, it certainly does not portray Him as a primitive warlike God who is mainly interested in destruction. His love is demonstrated throughout the entire Old Testament.

The New Testament emphasizes the love of God but it also speaks of God's judgment. Some of the harshest words of judgment recorded in the Bible were uttered by Jesus:

> But woe to you, scribes and Pharisees, hypocrites! For you shut up the kingdom of heaven against men; for you neither go in yourselves, nor do you allow those who are entering to go in (Matthew 23:13).

The Apostle Paul wrote to the church at Thessalonica about the judgment of God:

> When the Lord Jesus is revealed from heaven with His mighty angels, in flaming fire taking vengeance on those who do not know God, and on those who do not obey the gospel of our Lord Jesus Christ. These shall be punished with everlasting destruction from the presence of the Lord and from the glory of His power (2 Thessalonians 1:7-9).

When all the evidence is considered we find both the Old and New Testament give a consistent portrait of God. His love and compassion as well as His judgment can be found in the Old Testament, while His judgment upon sin and His compassion and love are clearly taught in the New Testament.

WHAT IS THE GRACE OF GOD?

The Bible speaks of the grace of God. What does this mean? How does it affect the believer? God's grace can be defined as "God's response to man's need." Grace can also be described mercy, loving-kindness, or unmerited favor.

From the first page of the Bible until the last we have examples of God's grace extended to people. In the Garden of Eden, after Adam and Eve brought sin into the world, God demonstrated His mercy by postponing the judgment upon them.

Since the time of Adam and Eve, everyone born into this world has been a sinner and possesses a nature that is spiritually dead. All of us need help. It is here that God has shown his grace or mercy to us.

God mercifully sent Jesus Christ to die for the sins of the world.

> For when we were still without strength, in due time Christ died for the ungodly. For scarcely for a righteous man will one die; yet perhaps for a good man someone would even dare to die. But God demonstrates His own love toward us, in that while we were still sinners, Christ died for us (Romans 5:6-8).

The death of Christ was His response to man's need to be delivered from sin and its consequences. When a person trusts Jesus for salvation it is by God's grace that he is saved.

For by grace you have been saved through faith, and
that not of yourselves; it is the gift of God, not of works,
lest anyone should boast (Ephesians 2:8,9).

Those who believe in Christ will not be judged but will
receive God's mercy and forgiveness.

When we speak about the grace of God we are referring
to the characteristic of God that shows mercy to mankind.
The entire Bible records God mercifully reaching out to
meet the needs of helpless humanity. His mercy is not a
response to works, but to repentance.

DOES THE BIBLE RECORD GOD SPEAKING TO MAN IN DREAMS?

The Bible mentions several ways in which God revealed Himself to mankind. One of the ways was through dreams and visions.

Then He said, 'Hear now My words: If there is a prophet among you, I, the Lord, make Myself known to him in a vision, and I will speak to him in a dream' (Numbers 12:6).

On one occasion God used a dream to speak to the patriarch Jacob:

Then he dreamed a dream, and behold a ladder was set up on the earth, and its top reached to heaven; and there the angels of God were ascending and descending on it. And behold, the Lord stood above it and said: 'I am the Lord God of Abraham your father and the God of Isaac; the land on which you lie I will give to you and your descendants' (Genesis 28:12,13).

It was through a dream that God told Joseph to take Mary, the mother of Jesus, as his wife:

But while he thought about these things, behold, an angel of the Lord appeared to him in a dream saying. 'Joseph, son of David, do not be afraid to take to you Mary your wife, for that which is conceived in her is of the Holy Spirit' (Matthew 1:20).

Visions

God has communicated to mankind through visions.

Now the Lord spoke to Paul in the night by a vision, 'Do not be afraid, but speak, and do not keep silent' (Acts 18:9).

God used dreams and visions, for the most part, to reveal His will to those who already believed in him. Dreams were not used to prove His existence to those who doubted.

Not a Guarantee

The Bible does not teach that every dream is a guarantee that do is trying to speak to a person. Scripture does speak about evil dreams and dreams of natural origin:

If there arises among you a prophet or a dreamer of dreams, and he gives you a sign or a wonder, and the sign or the wonder comes to pass, of which he spoke to you saying, 'Let us go after other gods which you have not known, and let us serve them,' you shall not listen to the words of that prophet or that dreamer of dreams, for the Lord your God is testing you to know whether you love the Lord your God with all your heart and with all your soul (Deuteronomy 13:1-3).

Therefore a dreamer who gives signs and wonders is not from God if he urges the people to go after other gods.

Natural Explanation

There can also be a natural explanation for dreams. The writer of Ecclesiastes said:

For the dream comes through much activity, and a fool's voice is known by his many words (Ecclesiastes 5:3).

Thus, given what the Bible says about dreams, one cannot assume that a dream with some spiritual content is necessarily from God. Dreams can be from God, from an evil source, or a mere natural activity of the mind.

CONCLUSION TO PART 3

After looking at what the Bible says about the way God revealed Himself in the past we can conclude:

1. God has created both the universe and human beings.

2. God did not create evil. Evil was brought about by Adam and Eve rebelling against God.

3. God has revealed Himself in history.

4. God's character is consistent in the way He deals with people and nations. His dealings are always fair.

We have seen that there is evidence for God's existence. We have also seen what the Bible has to say about His nature and about the things He has done in the past. This brings us to Part 4 of this book—God and the Individual. Do we really need God? What does He require of us? Does prayer work? This last section will answer these and other questions relating to God and the individual.

PART 4

GOD: HIS RELATIONSHIP TO US

For by grace you have been saved through faith,
and that not of yourselves; it is the gift of God.
—Ephesians 2:8

WHY DOES ANYONE NEED GOD?

Is having God in one's life a luxury or a necessity? Can we live a full life without God?

The Bible says that we do have a choice. We can choose to serve God or choose to disobey Him. But whether an individual chooses to reject or trust God, the Bible is clear that we all need God. He provides for us an identity, a purpose, and a destiny.

Identity

God tells who we are. We are here by design, not by chance. We have been made in the image of God.

> Then God said, 'Let Us make man in Our image, according to Our likeness; let them have dominion over the fish of the sea, over the birds of the air, and over the cattle, over all the earth and over creeping things that creeps on the earth' (Genesis 1:26).

Man was created in God's image. This means we have the ability to love, communicate, and think. We also have the chance to know God on a personal level. This separates us from the animal kingdom. The Bible puts man on an entirely different level. Man is not an animal. Animals do not have the ability to know and worship God. God gave man the assignment to have charge over the animal kingdom. Animals were created for man. God provides man with a genuine identity.

Purpose

The Bible not only gives us this identity, as a unique creation of God, it also gives us a purpose for living. We are here to glorify God with our lives. Within the pages of the Bible we have a guidebook on how we can relate to God and how we are to conduct ourselves with one another. God has promised to guide us:

> Trust in the Lord with all your heart, and lean not on your own understanding; in all your ways acknowledge Him, and He shall direct your paths (Proverbs 3:5,6).

We do not need to grope in the dark. God's Word is our guide that tells us God's plan and how we should live. When we have a relationship with the living God our lives take on a purpose.

Destiny

God also provides for us a destiny. We know that this life is not all that there is. Scripture promises a conscious existence beyond the grave. God provides for us the assurance that we will spend eternity in His presence.

> These things I have written to you who believe in the name of the Son of God, that you may know that you have eternal life (1 John 5:13).

He has made those who trust in Jesus joint heirs to all that is His.

> The Spirit Himself bears witness with our spirit that we are children of God, and if children, then heirs—heirs of God and joint heirs with Christ (Romans 8:16,17).

Those who reject God not only lose the present benefits in this life of having a God-given identity and a real purpose, they also will lose the eternal benefits by being separated from God. The Bible says:

> When the Lord Jesus is revealed from heaven with His mighty angels, in flaming fire taking vengeance on those who do not know God, and on those who do not obey the gospel of our Lord Jesus Christ. They shall be punished with everlasting destruction from the presence of the Lord and from the glory of His power (2 Thessalonians 1:7-9).

Having God in one's life is a necessity for living both now and for eternity. A person can only find true fulfillment in God through Jesus Christ.

IS MANKIND LOOKING FOR GOD?

Many times we have the picture that each individual is in a desperate search for God while God is reluctant to reveal Himself. The Bible, however, has just the opposite to say. God is actively seeking man while man is running from God. The story of the Bible is that of a loving God who is constantly seeking after wayward man.

After Adam and Eve sinned God immediately came looking for them in the Garden of Eden. Instead of welcoming God, Adam and Eve hid from Him.

> And when they heard the sound of the Lord God walking in the garden in the cool of the day, and Adam and his wife hid themselves from the presence of the Lord God among the trees of the garden (Genesis 3:8).

When the children of Israel were in bondage in Egypt God heard their cry and sent a deliverer named Moses.

> And the Lord said, 'I have surely seen the oppression of My people who are in Egypt, and have heard the cry because of their taskmasters, for I know their sorrows' (Exodus 3:7).

God Becomes Man

Jesus Christ, the eternal God, became a man in order to reveal what God is like and to bring lost humanity back to Himself. The New Testament declares:

For the Son of Man has come to seek and to save that which was lost (Luke 19:10).

Jesus came to earth to bring sinful man back to a right relationship with God. The Bible makes it clear that God is actively seeking after man.

However, man is not looking for God. The Scripture says: "There is none who seeks after God" (Romans 3:11).

Man Suppressing Truth

Moreover, the Scriptures say that man is holding down the truth of God:

For the wrath of God is revealed from heaven against all ungodliness and unrighteousness of men, who suppress the truth in unrighteousness (Romans 1:18).

The picture here is that man is actively suppressing the truth of God. Rather than wanting to know God, the Bible portrays man as running away from God.

A close examination of the Bible reveals that God is looking for man while man is running from God.

CAN A PERSON PLEASE GOD BY BEING GOOD?

Many people feel they have lived a life that will be good enough to get them to heaven. Since their life has been characterized by a certain degree of morality they assume God will accept them. But the Bible states otherwise. None of us, no matter how good we have been, are able to stand before God.

As it is written: there is none righteous, no, not one; there is none who understands; there is none who seeks after God (Romans 3:10).

For all have sinned and come short of the glory of God (Romans 3:23).

For the wages of sin is death (Romans 6:23).

There are many moral and upright people in the world who contribute much to the common good. But the Bible says that no matter how good someone is, no person is good enough to meet God's perfect standard.

Measured by God

The Scriptures teach that man is not to be measured by man but by God. When the creature is measured by the Creator he is found wanting. The psalmist said:

Who may ascend into the hill of the Lord? Or who may stand in His holy place? He who has clean hands and a pure heart, who has not lifted up his soul to an idol, nor sworn deceitfully (Psalm 24:3,4).

The Apostle Paul wrote:

But the Scripture has confined all under sin, that the promise by faith in Jesus Christ might be given to those who believe (Galatians 3:22).

None of us is in a position to please God by our own goodness. We need God's help to become part of God's family. God has provided that help in the person of Jesus Christ.

Jesus came to earth that we might know what God is like and what He requires of us. When Christ was asked by His disciples about doing works that would please God He made it clear what God wanted from mankind.

Then they said to Him, what shall we do, that we may work the works of God? Jesus answered and said to them, 'This is the work of God, that you believe in Him whom He has sent' (John 6:28,29).

The Bible is clear that we must put our faith in Christ as God's provision for our salvation. Jesus' death on the cross paid the penalty for our sin. We must accept that sacrifice by faith.

For God so loved the world that He gave His only begotten Son, that whoever believes in Him should not perish but have everlasting life (John 3:16).

Faith in Christ is the only way we can please God and enter into heaven. Our good works alone will never be sufficient.

TO WHOM DOES GOD GIVE ETERNAL LIFE?

One of the offers that God makes to man is the gift of eternal life. God's promise of eternal life includes living forever in God's presence in a loving relationship with Him. Jesus defined what it means to receive eternal life:

> And this is eternal life, that they may know You, the only true God, and Jesus Christ whom You have sent (John 17:3).

The reason God can offer this eternal relationship between Himself and the believer is because of the death of Christ. Jesus died on the cross for the sins of the world. He died as our substitute taking the punishment we deserved for our sins. He offers eternal life to everyone who accepts His sacrifice by faith. The requirement is belief in Jesus Christ. The Bible says,

> He who believes in the Son has everlasting life; and he who does not believe the Son shall not see life, but the wrath of God abides on him (John 3:36).

> That if you confess with your mouth the Lord Jesus and believe that God has raised Him from the dead, you will be saved. For with the heart one believes to righteousness, and with the mouth confession is made to salvation (Romans 10:9,10).

There is nothing any of us can do to earn eternal life—it is a free gift of God:

> For by grace you have been saved through faith, and that not of yourselves; it is the gift of God, not of works, lest anyone should boast (Ephesians 2:8,9)

God has done everything He can. The only thing stopping an individual from receiving eternal life is his own will. Each of us must choose whether we accept of reject God's gift.

Those who reject the gift of salvation will spend eternity apart from God and His presence. Though the unbelievers will exist eternally they will receive the judgment of God, not His blessings.

We conclude the following:

1. Eternal life consists of knowing God and spending forever in His presence.

2. God promises everlasting life to those who put their faith in Him.

3. Those who do not believe in Christ will exist eternally apart from the presence of God.

CAN GOD
FORGIVE ANYBODY?

Some people assume that God could never forgive them because their lives have been too corrupt. They do not believe God would have anything to do with them. Yet the Bible teaches that no matter how bad anyone has been, forgiveness is still possible. No one will be denied access to God because they have lived sinful lives.

God sent Christ to seek out and save sinners. Jesus said:

> I did not come to call the righteous, but sinners, to repentance (Matthew 9:13).

When a person comes humbly to God for forgiveness He has promised to forgive him no matter what he has done. Jesus said:

> All the Father gives Me will come to Me, and the one who comes to Me I will by no means cast out (John 6:37).

Complete

The forgiveness that God grants is complete.

> As far as the east is from the west, so far has He removed our transgressions from us (Psalm 103:12)

He will again have compassion on us, and will subdue our iniquities. You will cast all our sins into the depths of the sea (Micah 7:19).

We are told to forgive others as God has forgiven us.

And be kind to one another, tenderhearted, forgiving one another, just as God in Christ also forgave you (Ephesians 4:32).

Therefore we can say:

1. God has promised to forgive anybody who comes to Him.

2. God's forgiveness is based upon the righteousness of Jesus, not our own.

3. The forgiveness He offers is complete. He will not hold our sin against us any more.

4. We are told to forgive others as God has forgiven us.

DOES A PERSON HAVE TO APPROACH GOD BY FAITH?

From the first page of the Bible until the last, God commands that those who approach Him do it on the basis of faith in Him and His Word. The children of the first couple, Adam and Eve, were Cain and Abel. God commanded that they bring a sacrifice to Him by faith. The sacrifice made by Abel was acceptable to God while the one brought by Cain was not. The Bible gives us the reason:

> By faith Abel offered to God a more excellent sacrifice than Cain, through which he obtained witness that he was righteous (Hebrews 11:4).

The eleventh chapter of the Book of Hebrews lists people who lived during the Old Testament period whose lives pleased God. Their lives were characterized by faith. The writer to the Hebrews makes this summary statement.

> But without faith it is impossible to please Him, for he who comes to God must believe that He is and that He is a rewarder of those who diligently seek Him (Hebrews 11:6).

The Apostle Paul wrote to the church at Corinth:

> For we walk by faith, not by sight (2 Corinthians 5:7).

Scripture repeatedly states that it is faith that pleases God and all of us who approach Him and desire to have a relationship with Him must do it by faith.

Great Faith Needed?

There are people who are afraid to come to God because they do not have great faith. They feel they must wait until their faith increases before they can approach Him. But this is not the case. The emphasis in the Bible is not on the amount of faith that a person has, but rather the object of the faith. Jesus made this clear.

And the apostles said to the Lord, 'Increase our faith.' So the Lord said, 'If you have faith as a mustard seed, you can say to this mulberry tree, "Be pulled up by the roots and planted in the sea," and it would obey you' (Luke 17:5,6).

Much can be accomplished through a small amount of faith as long as the object of the faith is trustworthy. The God of the Bible is always emphasizing Himself as the believer's object of faith. He is the one who is able to do great things.

Call to Me, and I will answer you, and show you great and mighty things which you do not know (Jeremiah 33:3).

The greatest faith in the world, if it has a wrong object, is worthless. It is in whom you have your faith, not the quantity of faith that matters. The believer does not need great faith to please God. A person needs only a small amount of faith in our great God to approach Him.

Blind Faith?

The Bible encourages people to put their faith in God. Unfortunately, many people equate faith with a blind leap in the dark or wishful thinking. But the faith that the Bible requires is intelligent faith. It is neither blind nor irrational. Biblical faith is a committing trust with an object (God) who is worthy of our faith. No one is asked to sacrifice his intellect when he puts his faith in the God of the Bible.

This is true because Christian faith is based upon the solid foundation of what God has done in history. God has revealed Himself to man and this revelation is recorded in the Scriptures. The Bible tells us what God requires of us and that we are to respond to Him by faith. In doing so, we are not expected to stop thinking or to act irrationally.

Jesus emphasized that coming to God involves the mind as well as the heart and soul.

> You shall love the Lord your God with all your heart, with all your soul, and with all your mind (Matthew 22:37).

When Jesus had a conversation with one of the scribes He equated intelligence with knowing God.

> So when Jesus saw that he answered wisely, He said to him, 'You are not far from the kingdom of God (Mark 12:34).

The Apostle Paul encouraged people to investigate the claims of Christianity to see if they were true.

> Test all things; hold fast what is good (1 Thessalonians 5:21).

The reason the biblical writers could encourage a person to investigate the Christian faith was because they knew what they were recording was true. Simon Peter showed that the New Testament writers were aware of the difference between mythology and fact:

> For we did not follow cunningly devised fables when we made known to you the power and coming of our Lord Jesus Christ, but were eyewitnesses of His majesty (2 Peter 1:16).

Because the New Testament writers were eyewitnesses to the events they recorded, they knew what they were recording was accurate. They welcomed an honest investigation of the facts. Blind faith was never encouraged.

God does not expect us to act in faith toward Him unless that faith is an intelligent faith built upon the solid foundation of what God has done in history and what He has recorded in His Word.

WHAT KEEPS PEOPLE FROM BELIEVING IN GOD?

The Bible makes it clear that it is not lack of evidence that keeps people from believing in God. The evidence is available for all to see but most people do not bother to investigate the evidence.

The reasons people do not believe in God are many, but they can be broken down into two basic categories: pride and ignorance.

Pride

The sin of pride keeps people from believing in God. Humanity does not want to admit that there is something or someone greater than human beings in the universe. People want to be the master of their own fate, captain of their own salvation. The Bible speaks of the pride of man.

> These six things the Lord hates, yes, seven are an abomination to Him: a proud look (Proverbs 6:16,17).

Pride is the first sin mentioned in a list of things that God hates. It was the sin of pride that caused Lucifer to rebel against God and be cast out of heaven. It was pride that caused Cain to bring an offering of his own works to the Lord instead of the one God had commanded. From the beginning of time, pride has kept people from coming to God.

James warned about the foolishness of pride:

Come now, you who say, 'Today or tomorrow we will go
to such and such a city, spend a year there, buy and sell,
and make a profit;' whereas you do not know what will
happen tomorrow. For what is your life? It is even a vapor
that appears for a little time and then vanishes away.
Instead you ought to say, if the Lord wills, we shall live
and do this or that (James 4:13-15).

Though people may boast that they do not need God
the fact is that they cannot exist without Him. People make
plans as though they will live forever, but as James
reminds us no one is guaranteed that he will be alive
tomorrow.

Ignorance

Another reason the Bible gives for lack of trust in God
is ignorance. Jesus pointed out that "not knowing" is a
source of error when it comes to believing in God.

You are mistaken, not knowing the Scriptures nor the
power of God (Matthew 22:29).

The two things that characterize unbelief is ignorance
of both the Scripture and the power of God. People do not
know what the Bible says because they have not taken the
time to carefully study it. Furthermore, they do not
understand the nature and greatness of God's power.
The Bible says that man is deliberately ignorant.

For the wrath of God is revealed from heaven against
all ungodliness and unrighteousness of men, who
suppress the truth in unrighteousness (Romans 1:18).

There is none righteous, no, not one; there is none who
understands; there is none who seeks after God (Romans
3:10,11).

These verses teach that people are not seeking after
God but are actually running away from Him. They are
suppressing or "holding down" God's truth in
unrighteousness. They are ignorant of God because they
want to be ignorant.

We conclude the following concerning why people do
not believe in God:

1. There are many reasons people do not believe in God but it is not because of lack of evidence.

2. People do not believe because of pride or an ignorance of God's Word and His power.

3. Those who are ignorant of God want to be ignorant. They do not want to know Him.

CAN GOD READ
OUR THOUGHTS?

Does God know what we think? Can He read our thoughts? The Bible says that God does have the capacity to know what we are thinking:

O Lord, You have searched me and known me. You know my sitting down and my rising up; You understand my thoughts afar off. You comprehend my path and my lying down, and are acquainted with all my ways. For there is not a word on my tongue, but behold, O Lord, you know it altogether (Psalm 139:1-4).

God knows everything that we think. He also knows what we will say before the words go out of our mouth. He knows everything about us.

Because God knows our thoughts, the Bible encourages us to concentrate upon thinking the right things. The Apostle Paul wrote the church at Philippi:

Finally, brethren, whatever things are true, whatever things are noble, whatever things are just, whatever things are pure, whatever things are lovely, whatever things are of a good report, if there is any virtue and if there is anything praiseworthy—meditate on these things (Philippians 4:8).

What kind of things should fill our minds? The Bible says that we should put our thoughts upon God's word, His commandments, and His promises:

Blessed is the man who walks not in the counsel of the ungodly, nor stands in the path of sinners, nor sits in the seat of the scornful; but his delight is in the law of the Lord, and in His law he meditates day and night (Psalm 1:1,2).

The Bible promises spiritual prosperity for those who meditate upon the word of God:

He shall be like a tree planted by the rivers of water, that brings forth fruit in its season, whose leaf shall not wither; and whatever he does shall prosper (Psalm 1:3).

Therefore, it is important to think the right thoughts, for according to Scripture we become that which we think:

For as he thinks in his heart, so is he (Proverbs 23:7).

We conclude that:

1. God has the capacity to read our thoughts.

2. He also knows what words we will say before they are spoken.

3. Because of this we are instructed to think about things that are good.

4. The good things we are to think about are contained in God's Word.

5. The Bible promises spiritual prosperity for those who meditate upon God's Word and who put it into practice.

80

DOES GOD MANIPULATE OUR LIVES?

A question that is often asked concerns the destiny of our lives and the actions of God. Are we being manipulated by God? Do we have choice in the decisions that we make or is God pulling the strings?

The Bible teaches that we do have a choice; our lives are not being manipulated by God. The Scripture presents many situations where the people had a choice to serve the true God or to serve false gods. Joshua, the leader of Israel, said:

> And if it seems evil to you to serve the Lord, choose for yourselves this day whom you will serve (Joshua 24:15).

The prophet Elijah contested the false prophets of the god Baal. He said to the people:

> How long will you falter between two opinions? If the Lord is God, follow Him; but if Baal, then follow him (1 Kings 18:21).

God has said that it is His desire that people choose to place their faith in Him.

> The Lord is not slack concerning His promise, as some count slackness, but is longsuffering toward us, not willing that any should perish but that all should come to repentance (2 Peter 3:9).

He holds those accountable who reject His word.

> He who believes in the Son has everlasting life; and he who does not believe the Son shall not see life, but the wrath of God abides on him (John 3:36).

From these biblical examples we observe that God holds man responsible for the choices he makes. If God were merely manipulating us in everything that we do, it would not make sense to hold us responsible for our actions. Because we are held accountable for our deeds it is clear that we are not being manipulated. We are free to choose our own way.

We can sum up by concluding:

1. The actions we perform and the choices that we make are our own. We cannot blame God for not giving us the ability to choose to believe in Him.

2. The Bible teaches that God will hold us accountable for the choices that we make.

WHY DO WE HAVE TO PLAY BY GOD'S RULES

If we accept the fact that the Bible gives us God's rules for life, we are faced with the question: Why must we play by God's rules? Why can't we make up the rules?

To answer this question we must understand God's relationship with each person.

God's Universe

God is the Creator of the universe. He is our Creator. As the psalmist wrote:

> Know that the Lord, He is God; it is He who has made us, and not we ourselves; we are His people and the sheep of His pasture (Psalm 100:3).

Because God created all things He has established the physical laws of the universe. We are all bound by these rules and if we break them we will suffer the consequences. For example, if we do not eat, drink and breathe we will die. There is no alternative. We cannot expect to survive if we break the physical laws God has set in motion.

Likewise, God has established moral and spiritual laws which He asks us to obey. When we disobey these laws or ignore them we will have to suffer the consequences. God's laws—physical, moral and spiritual—were established by our heavenly Father for our good.

Rebelling against God and disregarding His commands means that we will miss the best in life that God has planned and offered to humanity—"the sheep of His pasture."

The psalmist spoke about those who rebel against God.

Why do the nations rage, and the people plot a vain thing? The kings of the earth set themselves, and the rulers take counsel against the Lord and against His anointed saying, 'Let us break their bonds in pieces and cast away their cords from us. He who sits in the heavens shall laugh; the Lord shall hold them in derision' (Psalm 2:1-4).

God's word explains that the obedience He requests is for our good, our blessing.

And now Israel, what does the Lord your God require of you, but to fear the Lord your God, to walk in all His ways and to love Him, to serve the Lord your God with all your heart and with all your soul, and to keep the commandments of the Lord and His statues which I command you (Deuteronomy 10:12,13).

IS GOD ABLE TO MEET OUR NEEDS

All of us have difficulties and troubles in this life. When we turn to God with these problems we need assurance that He is able to help us deal with them. Does the Bible indicate that God is adequate to meet the needs of those who believe in Him?

God is Able

We have already seen that God is not dependent upon anything for His existence. Because of this He is sufficient to meet any and all needs that we have.

Actually we need go no further than the first verse in the Bible to see that God has sufficient power to meet our needs.

In the beginning God created the heavens and the earth (Genesis 1:1).

This verse tells us that God created everything that there is. This establishes His great power and creative ability. If God is powerful enough to create the universe, He certainly is able to meet the needs of those who live in it. The Scriptures speak of this power.

Whenever I am afraid, I will trust in You. In God (I will praise His word), in God I have put my trust; I will not fear. What can flesh do to me? (Psalm 56:3,4).

The Bible consistently testifies that God is more than adequate to deal with any situation we may face. John the evangelist told his readers they had nothing to fear because the Lord was with them:

> You are of God, little children, and have overcome them, because He who is in you is greater than he who is in the world (1 John 4:4).

No Need to Fear

We need not fear any human being or angelic power. The Apostle Paul wrote to the believers in Rome:

> What then shall we say to these things? If God is for us, who can be against us? (Romans 8:31).

The Bible says that God has provided a solution to any problem that believers may face:

> No temptation has overtaken you except such as is common to man; but God is faithful, who will not allow you to be tempted beyond what you are able, but with the temptation will also make the way of escape, that you may be able to bear it (1 Corinthians 10:13).

God has promised to meet all our needs:

> And my God shall supply all your need according to His riches in glory by Christ Jesus (Philippians 4:19).

Although God has promised to meet our needs we must be careful not to assume that He has given us a blank check. God does not give us everything that we ask for. But He does supply our needs. Moreover, if we get ourselves in a difficult situation, God has indeed promised to provide a way out. However this does not mean that we can escape the consequences of our wrong doing. The Bible says:

> Do not be deceived, God is not mocked; for whatever a man sows, that he will also reap (Galatians 6:7).

For example, a thief may repent of his stealing and be forgiven by God but he still must pay the penalty for his crime. We can be forgiven but there are temporal consequences to our sin.

We can thus conclude:

1. God is powerful enough to supply all our needs.

2. He has promised to meet the needs of those who believe in Him. He has not promised to give us everything we ask for.

3. God has promised a solution to every difficult situation but we will not escape the temporal consequences of our wrongdoing.

WHY DO PEOPLE SUFFER?

Does the Bible give any reasons why people go through times of suffering?

Although the Scriptures do not give a complete explanation of why people suffer it does provide some solutions and comfort.

Not Original Intention

The Bible teaches that suffering is an intrusion into the universe that God has made. It was not His original intention that people suffer. When God created the universe everything was good.

> And God saw everything that He had made, and indeed it was very good (Genesis 1:31).

Result of Sin

Suffering entered into God's universe as a result of sin. This occurred when Adam and Eve disobeyed God at the prompting of the devil. Because of their disobedience God pronounced judgment upon them. This included that they would suffer in this life.

> To the woman He said: 'I will greatly multiply your sorrow and your conception; in pain you shall bring forth children; your desire shall be for your husband, and he

shall rule over you.' Then to Adam He said, . . . 'Cursed is
the ground for your sake; in toil you shall eat of it all the
days of your life. Both thorns and thistles it shall bring
forth for you, and you shall eat the herb of the field. In the
sweat of your face you shall eat bread till you return to the
ground, for out of it you were taken; for dust you are, and
to dust you shall return' (Genesis 3:16-19).

If we are to understand suffering we must realize that
human responsibility is involved in much of the suffering
that goes on. We suffer on our own account or because of
what others have done to us. We should not blame God for
the suffering that we bring upon ourselves or that others
cause.

But no matter who is responsible for suffering the fact
is that we still suffer. How can we experience relief from
that suffering?

The Bible teaches that Jesus came to relieve the
problem of human suffering. Jesus spoke of one of the
purposes of His coming.

The Spirit of the Lord is upon Me, because He has
anointed Me to preach the gospel to the poor. He has sent
Me to heal the brokenhearted, to preach deliverance to
the captives and recovery of sight to the blind, to set at
liberty those who are oppressed (Luke 4:18).

Jesus also taught that there was something worse
than physical suffering.

And I say to you, My friends, do not be afraid of those
who kill the body, and after that have no more that they
can do. But I will show you whom you should fear: fear
Him who, after He has killed, has power to cast into hell;
yes, I say to you, fear Him! (Luke 12:4,5).

The Bible teaches that Jesus suffered on our behalf.

For when we were still without strength, in due time
Christ died for the ungodly (Romans 5:6).

Because of Jesus' sacrifice on our behalf God will
someday put an end to suffering.

And I saw a new heaven and a new earth, for the first
heaven and the first earth had passed away. . . And I
heard a loud voice from heaven saying, 'Behold, the
tabernacle of God is with men and He will dwell with them,

and they shall be His people, and God Himself will be with them and be their God. And God shall wipe away every tear from their eyes; there shall be no more death, nor sorrow, nor crying; and there shall be no more pain, for the former things have passed away. Then He who sat on the throne said, 'Behold, I make all things new' (Revelation 21:1,3-5).

Therefore we conclude the following with regard to suffering:

1. When God created the universe there was no sickness or suffering.

2. Suffering came as a result of man's sin. It was not something God built into the universe.

3. Jesus came to relieve the problem of suffering.

4. He taught that there was something worse than physical suffering.

5. Jesus suffered and died on our behalf so that one day there would be no more suffering.

84

HOW CAN A PERSON LIVE WITH SUFFERING?

First of all we must understand that suffering is something that all of us, believer and unbeliever alike, will experience in this life. Even Jesus Christ suffered. In fact, His suffering was the means God used to accomplish our salvation. The Bible does not promise believers escape from suffering. Simon Peter wrote:

Beloved, do not think it strange concerning the fiery trial which is to try you, as though something strange happened to you; but rejoice to the extent that you partake of Christ's sufferings, that when His glory is revealed, you may also be glad with exceeding joy (1 Peter 4:12,13).

Sometimes the believer will seemingly suffer more than the unbeliever. This is because the unbelieving world hates those who stand for God's truth. Jesus said:

If the world hates you, you know that it hated Me before it hated you. If you were of the world, the world would love its own. Yet because you are not of the world, but I chose you out of the world, therefore the world hates you (John 15:18,19).

God Will Be With Us

However God has made promises to the believer when he is suffering. King David said:

Yea, though I walk through the valley of the shadow of death, I will fear no evil; for You are with me; Your rod and Your staff; they comfort me (Psalm 23:4).

God has said:

I will never leave you nor forsake you (Hebrews 13:5).

God has promised to be with and comfort those who suffer. Though God has promised to be with us we may not always understand why we are suffering. God has not obligated Himself to tell us why we suffer but He asks us to trust Him through our sufferings.

After experiencing tremendous suffering, the biblical character Job reached the point of surrendering himself to God. He then humbly said:

I know that you can do everything, and that no purpose of Yours can be withheld from You. You asked, 'Who is this who hides counsel without knowledge?' Therefore I have uttered what I did not understand, things too wonderful for me, which I did not know . . . I abhor myself, and repent in dust and ashes (Job 42:2,3,6).

We must also remember that if it were not for the suffering freely endured by Jesus Christ, we would have no salvation from our sins.

Therefore we conclude the following with regard to suffering:

1. Those who believe in the God of the Bible are not promised relief from suffering in this life.

2. Sometimes believers seemingly suffer more than non-believers.

3. God has made promises to be with the believer who is suffering.

4. We may not always understand why we suffer.

5. Jesus' suffering makes our salvation possible.

DOES GOD ANSWER ALL
OUR PRAYERS?

Some people feel that their prayers go unanswered. They asked God for some specific thing and that thing was not granted. Does God answer all our prayers? Upon what basis does He answer them?

God Hears Our Prayers

The Bible says that God does hear prayer. Jesus encouraged people to pray.

Then He spoke a parable to them, that men ought to pray and not lose heart (Luke 18:1).

James also encouraged the people to pray:

You do not have because you do not ask (James 4:2).

But many times the answer to prayer is no for God does not promise to give us everything we ask. He has promised to meet all our needs.

And my God shall supply all your need according to His riches in glory by Christ Jesus (Philippians 4:19).

However God has clearly stated that the basis that He can be approached in prayer is through His Son Jesus Christ. He is the mediator between God and man.

For there is one God and one Mediator between God and men, the Man Christ Jesus (1 Timothy 2:5).

The Bible pictures Jesus constantly interceding on behalf of the believer:

Therefore He is able to save to the uttermost those who come to God through Him, since He ever lives to make intercession for them (Hebrews 7:25).

God's holy nature makes it impossible for sinful individuals to have access to Him. This is because there is a great gulf between sinful humanity and a holy God. The Apostle Paul said concerning God:

Who alone has immortality, dwelling in unapproachable light, whom no man has ever seen or can see (1 Timothy 6:16).

God's holy nature makes it impossible for sinful man to have access to him. That is why Christ is needed as our go-between, or mediator. We have no choice but to approach God on that basis.

Those who pray without the mediating work of Christ have no access to God the Father. Their prayers have no basis on which to be heard. The only legitimate prayer that an unbeliever can pray to God is a prayer of mercy. When he asks God's forgiveness for his sins and accepts Jesus as his savior, he then has access to God through Jesus, His Son.

We need to ask God the same thing that Jesus' disciples asked him: "Lord, teach us to pray" (Luke 11:1).

We conclude by saying:

1. God encourages us to pray.

2. Only through Christ can our prayers be heard.

3. Those apart from Christ need to pray for mercy.

4. Believers are guaranteed answers to all their prayers but are not guaranteed to get everything they ask for.

WILL GOD CONDEMN
SOMEONE FOR FAILING?

When people commit their lives to God they have a normal fear of failing. Some worry that God will condemn them for not being able to keep that commitment. But God has promised not only to save the person from sin, but to keep him saved.

Therefore He is also able to save to the uttermost those who come to God through Him, since He ever lives to make intercession for them (Hebrews 7:25).

Secure in Christ

In a triumphant note the Apostle Paul wrote the church in Rome that those who believe in Christ are secure in Him:

Who is he who condemns? It is Christ who died, and furthermore is also risen, who is even at the right hand of God, who also makes intercession for us. Who shall separate us from the love of Christ? Shall tribulation, or distress, or persecution, or famine, or nakedness, or peril, or sword? (Romans 8:34,35).

The reason we are secure in Him is because Jesus is both the author and finisher of our faith.

Looking unto Jesus the author and finisher of our faith, who for the joy that was set before Him endured the cross, despising the shame, and has sat down at the right hand of the throne of God (Hebrews 12:2).

Jesus sat down because the work of salvation is finished. We only need to trust Him for it.

He has also given His word that He will be with us always. As human beings we have the need for someone to be by our side for support. The Bible tells us that we are not alone. God has promised never to leave us,

For He Himself has said, 'I will never leave you nor forsake you' (Hebrews 13:5).

Believers should not worry about failing to keep the commitment they make to God through Christ, because God has the power to keep that person from falling. And God promises that He will do exactly that.

HOW CAN A PERSON PREPARE FOR DEATH?

All of us have to face the fact that we will eventually die. What happens to a person after death? The writer of Ecclesiastes, like the rest of us, wondered about what happens to people when they die.

> For what happens to the sons of men also happens to beasts; one thing befalls them: as one dies, so dies the other, surely, they all have one breath; man has no advantage over beasts, for all is vanity. All go to one place: all are from the dust, and all return to dust (Ecclesiastes 3:19,20).

Hope

From an observational point of view we do not know what happens to a person after they die. We bury their body and it returns to dust. From these verses it would seem as though death is the end.

But a further study of God's Word, the Bible, reveals that death is not the end of existence, it is just the beginning of eternity. There is hope of eternal life for those who die.

Jesus promised everlasting life to those who believe in Him. "Because I live, you will live also" (John 14:19).

The Apostle Paul wrote to the church at Thessalonica regarding the state of those who had died.

But I do not want you to be ignorant, brethren, concerning those who have fallen asleep, lest you sorrow as others who have no hope. For if we believe that Jesus died and rose again, even so God will bring with Him those who sleep in Jesus (1 Thessalonians 4:13,14).

The Apostle Paul says it is proper for people to sorrow for those who have died. But we are not to sorrow as the unbelievers do for we have a hope beyond the grave.

The Bible promises a new body for those who trust God.

For we know that if our earthly house, this tent, is destroyed, we have a building from God, a house not made with hands, eternal in the heavens (2 Corinthians 5:1).

For this corruptible must put on incorruption, and this mortal must put on immortality (1 Corinthians 15:53).

Because the Bible promises eternal life in God's presence for those who trust Christ there are things people can do to prepare for death. The first step is obvious. Preparation for death and eternal life requires faith in Jesus Christ.

The believer can then prepare for death by realizing that God has a purpose and a plan for his life. The psalmist trusted God to be with Him through the experience of life as well as death.

Yea, though I walk through the valley of the shadow of death, I will fear no evil; for you are with me (Psalm 23:4).

We conclude:

1 The Bible offers hope for those who are facing death.

2 Those who believe in Christ are promised everlasting life and a new body for eternity.

IS THERE A SECOND CHANCE AFTER DEATH FOR PEOPLE TO BELIEVE IN GOD?

Will people who have died have another chance to receive God's forgiveness in the next life? Is there a second chance for humanity?

The Bible says no. This life is the only one we will have to make a decision to trust God or to disobey Him.

The Bible teaches that when a believer dies he goes immediately to be with the Lord.

We are confident, yes, well pleased rather to be absent from the body and to be present with the Lord (2 Corinthians 5:8).

Those who do not believe go to a place of judgment.

He who believes the Son has everlasting life; and he who does not believe the Son shall not see life, but the wrath of God abides on him (John 3:36).

It is better to enter the kingdom of God with one eye, than having two eyes, to be cast into hell fire (Mark 9:47).

The Bible does not teach about a temporary state of the dead where people still have a chance to decide for God. The Scripture says that judgment comes after death.

And as it is appointed for men to die once, but after this the judgment (Hebrews 9:27).

Therefore, the Bible says concerning a second chance:

1. Those who die believing in God's promises will go immediately to be with Him.

2. The Bible is clear that judgment comes after death. the people who have not believed in God's promises will be sent to judgment immediately upon dying.

3. The Scripture does not teach or infer any temporary state of the dead where the person will have another chance to believe.

WILL GOD EVENTUALLY ALLOW EVERYONE INTO HEAVEN?

There are some people who contend that because God is a God of love that He will eventually allow everyone into heaven. This view, known as universalism, considers hell a temporary place of punishment. But the Bible clearly teaches otherwise. The judgment of hell is as eternal as is eternal life to those who believe.

And these will go away into everlasting punishment, but the righteous into eternal life (Matthew 25:46).

Jesus pointed out that there would be no crossover between heaven and hell. In the parable of the rich man who was in hell. Abraham responded to the pleas of the rich man by saying,

Between us and you there is a great gulf fixed, so that those who want to pass from here to you cannot, nor can those from there pass to us (Luke 16:26).

If it were true that God would eventually send everyone to heaven, then God would be forcing people to be in His presence against their will. Heaven would consist of many people who would not want to be there. The unbeliever's nature would still be in rebellion with God.

If universalism were true, then an obvious logical difficultly arises. Why does God allow the present world to suffer so much pain and sorrow if everyone will be converted by force?

The idea of universalism, that everyone will eventually end up in heaven, is not true because God gave each person the privilege of choice. We can accept or reject God's gift of eternal life.

We conclude:

1. The Bible clearly teaches heaven and hell are two distinct places. It is impossible to cross over from one to the other.

2. If universalism were true then people would end up in heaven against their will. They would not want to worship and serve God.

3. The present pain and sorrow that humanity experiences would not make sense if God were going to convert everyone.

HOW CAN SOMEONE FIND GOD'S BEST FOR THEIR LIFE?

Everyone wants to live the best life possible. How can a person find God's best for his life?

The Bible tells us that God wants to give us our heart's desires:

Delight yourself also in the Lord, and He shall give you the desires of your heart (Psalm 37:4).

What steps must we take to find God's best for our lives?

Trust Christ

The first thing God expects from us is belief. We are to believe that He exists and that He has revealed Himself in the person of Jesus Christ. It is only through faith in Jesus that a person can come to God.

Nor is there salvation in any other, for there is no other name under heaven given among men by which we must be saved (Acts 4:12).

Once a person has made the step of faith by believing in Christ as Savior, he then becomes a child of God. Then the individual begins to develop a personal relationship with God. To do this, the believer must take time to study God's Word. The believer is instructed to study the Bible:

Be diligent to present yourself approved to God, a worker who does not need to be ashamed, rightly dividing the word of truth (2 Timothy 2:15).

A careful study of the Scripture will help the person determine what it is that God expects from him. The Bible records God's commands and the promises He makes to those who trust Him.

Faith

The main thing that God is looking for in the believer is faith. He has promised to bless those who trust Him.

Trust in the Lord with all your heart, and lean not on your own understanding; in all your ways acknowledge Him, and He shall direct your paths (Proverbs 3:5,6).

The believer continually acknowledges God and receives those good gifts the Lord has promised. Believing God, developing a personal relationship with Him based on faith in Christ—these are the steps required for experiencing God's best for life.

Thus for a person finds God's best for his life he must do the following:

1. Believe in Christ as his Savior.

2. The believer should then develop a close, intimate, communicating, personal relationship with God. He does this by studying God's Word to find out what God requires and then to believe and apply the promises God has given.

CONCLUSION TO PART 4

From what the Bible has to say about God and the individual we conclude:

1. We all need God.

2. God has made it possible for us to know Him.

3. The way we can know God personally is through His Son Jesus Christ.

4. Those who believe in Jesus become part of God's family.

5. Those who reject Christ will spend eternity apart from God.

6. It is God's desire that all of us know Him.

7. Once a person has made a commitment to Christ He can find out what God requires of him by studying the Bible, praying, meeting regularly with other Christians, and acting upon His commitment.

SUMMARY

In our study of what the Bible says about God we have discovered that there is ample evidence to believe that God exists and that He has revealed Himself to mankind. God has shown Himself to be a good God having man's best interests always in mind.

God has made a way by which we may know Him through the person of Jesus Christ. Jesus' death upon the cross for the sins of the world makes it possible for us to enter into a personal relationship with God.

It is the responsibility of the individual to accept, by faith, the sacrifice Jesus made on each person's behalf. Those who trust Him receive everlasting life. Those who do not believe will exist eternally apart from God's presence. The choice is yours. Jesus' offer is still being made today:

Come to Me, all you who labor and are are heavy laden, and I will give you rest. Take My yoke upon you and learn from Me, for I am gentle and lowly in heart, and you will find rest for your souls. For My yoke is easy and My burden is light (Matthew 11:28-30).

ABOUT THE AUTHOR

Don Stewart

Don Stewart is one of the most successful writers in the country having authored or co-authored over twenty books. These include *You Be The Judge, The Coming Temple* and *Ten Reasons To Trust the Bible.*

Don's writings have also achieved international success. Twenty-four of his titles have been translated into different languages including Chinese, Finnish, Polish, Spanish, German, and Portuguese.

Don received his undergraduate degree at Biola University majoring in Bible. He received a masters degree from Talbot Theological Seminary graduating with the highest honors. Don is a member of the national honor society, Kappa Tau Epsilon.

Don is also an internationally known apologist, a defender of the historic Christian faith. In his defense of Christianity he has traveled to over thirty countries speaking at colleges, universities, churches, seminars, and retreats. His topics include the evidence for Christianity, the identity of Jesus Christ, the challenge of the cults, and the relationship of the Bible and science.

Because of his international success as an author and speaker, Don's various books have generated sales of over one million copies.

Other Books By Don Stewart from Dart Press

You Be The Judge: Is Christianity True?

Ten Reasons To Trust The Bible (formerly titled The Ten Wonders Of The Bible).

The Coming Temple (with Chuck Missler)

Basic Bible Study Series

* What Everyone Needs To Know About **Jesus**

* What Everyone Needs To Know About **The Holy Spirit**

* What Everyone Needs To Know About **The Bible**

To order books call toll free 1-800-637-5177

Books Coming From Don Stewart in 1992

In Search of the Lost Ark: The Quest for the Ark of the Covenant

Basic Bible Study Series

* What The Bible Says About **Science**

* What The Bible Says About **The Future**